DATE DUE

Facilitating Community and Decision-Making Groups

The Professional Practices in Adult Education and Human Resource Development Series explores issues and concerns of practitioners who work in the broad range of settings in adult and continuing education and human resource development.

The books are intended to provide information and strategies on how to make practice more effective for professionals and those they serve. They are written from a practical viewpoint and provide a forum for instructors, administrators, policy makers, counselors, trainers, managers, program and organizational developers, instructional designers, and other related professionals.

Editorial correspondence should be sent to the Editor-in-Chief:

Michael W. Galbraith
c/o Krieger Publishing Company
P. O. Box 9542
Melbourne, FL 32902–9542

Facilitating Community and Decision-Making Groups

Allen B. Moore
and
James A. Feldt

KRIEGER PUBLISHING COMPANY
MALABAR, FLORIDA
1993

Original Edition 1993

Printed and Published by
KRIEGER PUBLISHING COMPANY
KRIEGER DRIVE
MALABAR, FLORIDA 32950

Library of Congress Cataloging-In-Publication Data

Moore, Allen B.
    Facilitating community and decision making groups / by Allen B.
Moore and James A. Feldt.
        p.   cm.
    Includes bibliographical references and index.
    ISBN 0-89464-650-8
    1. Community organization—Planning.   2. Decision-making, Group.
3. Community leadership.   I. Feldt, James A.   II. Title.
HM131.M614   1992
302.3—dc20   92-16669
                                                            CIP

10 9 8 7 6 5 4 3 2

CONTENTS

PART I.

THE BEFORE PHASE OR THE DESIGN DANCE

PART II.

THE DURING PHASE OR WHAT
YOU DO AT THE FACILITATED SESSION

PART III.

THE AFTER PHASE OR WHAT YOU DO
AFTER YOU THOUGHT YOU WERE DONE

PREFACE

Why write this book? We find that the need for facilitation of community and decision groups is dramatically greater now than it was in the past and we believe that the need will grow larger. This is due to a variety of factors. The retraction of federal programs and initiatives which occurred under the Reagan administration left states and local communities to deal with problems on their own. Now the increasing fiscal plight of the states has necessarily left the local communities with trying to address issues and problems that once would have been passed on to the state or federal governments. Additionally, the nature of many of the problems being faced seems to have changed; the problems seem to be more complex, more wicked, and require the mutual attention of several parties in order to be addressed. The need to bring multiple parties together to work out a common agenda relative to a problem means that ways must be found to assist groups where no one person or party ought to clearly be in charge. The proper method to address many of these problems also appears to have shifted. It has shifted from a reliance upon technical experts who can provide the technically correct answer, to a need to involve the affected parties into discovering more than one answer and building a sense of ownership in and motivation to follow through on an answer. Facilitation of community and decision-making groups is a way to assist in finding more creative responses to problems, of involving parties in creating and owning their own solutions, and, in the long term, transferring to communities and groups the enhanced ability to work cooperatively. Facilitation is a key component, and perhaps the key component, in group problem solving (Bostrom, Anson, & Clawson, 1991). We write this book, therefore, to enable more people to fulfill this function for communities and decision groups.

USE OF PERSONAL
EXPERIENCES AND EXAMPLES

We have used examples, scenarios, real situations, and, where appropriate, incorporated research results to illustrate points in the book. Obviously, we have changed the names of people, places, events, and communities "to protect the innocent," but have illustrated the emotion, frustration, or accomplishment of a group as they make decisions and solve problems. We have presented checklists, questions, and report examples to specify processes, procedures, and criteria for action. It has been our objective to incorporate real examples of events, results, successes, and failures or errors in the book to more clearly demonstrate facilitation planning and activities.

During the past 6 years we (individually and collectively) have worked with over 130 different groups to assist them in problem solving, decision making, and planning. Our role has been one of enabling, assisting, designing structures, and engaging group members in doing things to solve local, regional, and statewide issues and challenges. Based upon our knowledge of the professional literature in political science, organization development, small group processes, leadership, and program planning for group learning, but even more important, based upon our experience we view facilitators as:

- helping a group stay on task while being neutral to the content;
- being of service to a group;
- enabling a group to see other action options;
- designing a structured process with a group to analyze a problem situation; and
- assisting a group through a decision-making process.

Often we work with community groups such as the board of directors of a nonprofit organization or the membership of a community group. These groups clearly have some shared history and previous experiences of working (or failing to work) together. However, we work with representatives of different organizations and groups in a community who come together for the first time and, therefore, have no history of working together as a group.

For the past 4 years we have taught 2-day seminars on facilitation skills, a 2-day session on basic skills and then another 2 days for advanced issues. People attending these seminars are interested in how to handle requests for facilitation, design the process with local leaders, establish the contract, conduct the session, and follow-up with individuals and groups to check on action plans. In preparation for these seminars and when getting ready to conduct community meetings we have searched the professional literature, for example, articles, books, journals, magazines, and reports, to locate ideas, techniques, methods, and guidelines for facilitation. We have not been able to locate a document that meets our specific needs about facilitating new groups or preexisting groups for community problem solving and decision making.

We have referenced all ideas that we think came from other sources. Much of what we are reporting in this document is from first hand experience: listening to the clients' or groups' "worst nightmare of a meeting"; reflecting upon our experience in working with other groups; searching out ideas and procedures from the professional and commercial literature; and trying out small and large group techniques to achieve client expectations. So, this book is an effort on our part to share these experiences and the lessons we have derived from them. We hope that others will:

• learn about how to facilitate a group and
• see, as we have, that facilitation and group processes are powerful problem-solving techniques with wide application.

ACKNOWLEDGMENTS

We wish to thank the many people with whom we have had the privilege to work in small and large groups during facilitated sessions. We also appreciate the patience, support, and opportunities provided us through the Institute of Community and Area Development (ICAD), by the director Joe Whorton, and by our colleagues and fellow facilitators at ICAD.

Special thanks are due Mr. J. Wesley Wynens who critiqued parts of the book including the book flow, community planning session, and action plan figures. Several people assisted us by reading various drafts of the book including, Ms. Claudia Huff, Ms. Carlton Crowley, Dr. Susan Jenkins, Dr. John Rohrbaugh, Mr. Sam Mitchell, and Dr. Bradley Courtenay. Thanks also to Dr. Carol Downs who said we could and should write up what we were doing about facilitation.

While Jim Feldt did most of the word processing work for our writing team, we want to acknowledge frequent assistance from Ms. Sandy Phillips and Ms. Michelle Dillard.

Finally, we dedicate this book to those who have helped us grow, develop, and learn our trade: our teachers, colleagues, associates, and clients. Additionally, to single out two special people, this is for Anne and Pam.

THE AUTHORS

Allen B. Moore is associate professor of adult education. He is on staff at both the Department of Adult Education in the College of Education and the Institute of Community and Area Development at The University of Georgia in Athens. He received his B.S. degree (1964) in forest management, a masters degree (1968) in forestry and his Ed. D. (1970) in adult education from North Carolina State University at Raleigh.

Moore's main research and writing activities have focused on human capital development related to participation in continuing education, staff development, and community adult education. He has written numerous journal articles, book chapters, and monographs on career development, rural adult education, resources for handicapped adults, and human capital investments. He is an active member in the American Association of Adult Continuing Education (AAACE) and the Georgia Adult Education Association (GAEA), from which he received in 1989 the distinguished service award. Since 1986 he has conducted numerous instructional programs for members of non-profit community boards in Georgia. He has chaired the publications committee of the Adult Education Association USA (1980) and the publications committee of GAEA (1986–88) and served on the 1990–1992 publications committee of GAEA.

James A. Feldt is a public service associate with the Institute of Community and Area Development (ICAD), a service unit of The University of Georgia. He is also an adjunct faculty member of the Political Science Department, teaching in the Public Administration program. He holds B.A. (1974),

M.P.A. (1977), and D.P.A. (1986) degrees from the State University of New York at Albany.

Feldt's areas of specialization in his graduate studies were in policy analysis, with emphasis on quantitative approaches to inform decision making, and organization behavior. What has come to be his life's work is the intersection of those two areas, that is, assisting groups in problem-solving activities. His group decision work uses knowledge of decision types and how to structure approaches to addressing those types with a sensitive management of group dynamics and process. Feldt initially developed this knowledge base and these skills while completing his graduate studies. He served as the first facilitator for the Decision Techtronics Group, a consulting entity providing decision conferencing, located within SUNY Albany's Graduate School of Public Affairs. Since joining ICAD in 1985 Feldt has helped to infuse the decision-conferencing technology throughout ICAD and has worked with a large and diverse range of Georgia organizations, committees, task forces, and ad hoc groups.

INTRODUCTION

FACILITATION IN A PROBLEM-SOLVING AND DECISION-MAKING CONTEXT

We have drawn upon a number of sources to guide our use of facilitation for group decision making and problem solving. The sources help to characterize and distinguish facilitation from teaching, training, and leadership.

Facilitation is the role of helping participants to learn in an experimental group (Heron, 1989). An experimental group is one in which learning takes place through active involvement of the whole person—as a spiritual, thinking, feeling, choosing, energetically and physically embodied being.

In Wheelan's book, *Facilitating Training Groups*, (1990) there is no specific definition of facilitation or facilitating, rather the process is discussed by using case situations where a *trainer* makes decisions about how to work with a group depending upon its skills and comfort level. We especially like how she used beginning, middle (during), and ending as a framework for presenting intervention skills for trainers.

Galbraith (1991) writes about facilitating adult learning in the context of guiding, mentoring, and helping learners " . . . explore new intellectual territory" (p. ix). He points out a complex set of variables that interact to create a condition of unpredictability which increases the need for facilitators to be flexible and adaptable in order to accomplish stated goals or expectations. The key to individuals or groups achieving their goals appears to be related to flexibility, as opposed to a rigidity, in the learning process.

Rees (1991) writes about using facilitation skills to lead work teams. Business leaders are beginning to engage employees in more management functions. This trend is also related to reducing middle management positions thereby providing opportunities for individuals and work teams to direct and manage themselves. Facilitation in this context, according to Rees, is not delegating or controlling others, or presiding at meetings, or presenting information. It is the act of leading others to participate, to use group processes for productivity and satisfaction in the work place. The facilitating leader's role is that of: "listener, questioner, group process director, teacher, consensus builder, sharer of goal setting and decision making, and empowerer of others" (Rees, 1991, p. 21).

Fisher and Ellis (1990) describe zero-history groups which come together for the first time to address a particular purpose. They examine leaderless group discussions in which through a natural process, someone within the group assumes responsibility for keeping the group on track with a minimum of authority. This person can observe and shape the development of group identity, wherein the group becomes more than a mere collection of individuals as it works towards a specific goal, decision, plan or strategy.

Brookfield (1986) cites principles for effective practice regarding facilitation of adult learning. These include:

- adults need to be voluntary participants in the activity;
- participants must be respected by others for their unique contributions;
- facilitation has to be a collaborative enterprise;
- there should be a continuous process of activity, reflection, collaboration, new activity, new reflection, and so on; and
- the aim of facilitation should be empowerment, where adults can learn, do, act, reflect, judge, problem solve, decide, and so on as they determine what is best for them.

These basic principles are related to how facilitation of adults in zero-history groups are helped (facilitated) to make decisions and problem solve for their community, organization or collective.

Kayser (1990) talks about the " . . . facilitator as a person who helps a group free itself from internal obstacles or difficulties so that it may more efficiently and effectively pursue the achievement of its desired outcomes for a given meeting" (pp. 12–13). Kayser's approach is somewhat different from others who are writing about what the facilitator should do with a group. He sees facilitation being the responsibility of all those attending a meeting function or event. If participants are aware of these roles, activities, and responsibilities anyone attending the meeting can become the facilitator or group leader.

Facilitation of Community and Decision-Making Groups

From all of the above descriptions, what is or is not considered facilitation and why? Based upon our educational background, training, and experience (during the past 6 years) with a university-based service unit we find ourselves identifying with several of these authors but no author exclusively. The guide we use for facilitation (Brookfield, 1986; VanGundy, 1988; Huber, 1980; Heron, 1989) includes voluntary participation by those individuals and groups who may make decisions, those who will be affected by the decision, and those who might be opposed to the decision. Our experience indicates that if all parties are involved early in the decision-making process the decision is of better quality and it can be supported by a cross section of the community (Ashby, 1958; McGrath, 1984). Participant involvement is based upon collaborative efforts to reach consensus rather than in a competitive style. Group process procedures are used to engage individuals in idea generation, critical reflection and analysis of options, and selection of action plans. The process is designed to empower individuals and the group to look at situations and problems in a new or different view, to incorporate information and emotion from many perspectives, and to make decisions in an informed setting.

Definition of Often Used Terms

In this section we provide definitions of terms that we use throughout the book. These are not highly technical or arcane definitions. Our intent, simply, is to be very clear about what we mean by these terms.

Facilitator

A person who serves as the director and tracker of the group's discussions, deliberations, and process. This person does his or her best to remain neutral. He or she is not involved in the content discussion of the group. This person is, however, a deliberate manipulator of the process and flow of the group's work. He or she manipulates what the group does so as to maximize full participation, to minimize individuals dominating or interrupting the group, and to optimize the group's performance and satisfaction. Note that the word *manipulate* is consciously used here not to call up all the evil connotations but for its precise meaning of "to manage or utilize skillfully" (*Webster's Seventh New College Dictionary*, 1972).

Groups

Clients or participants who come together to deal with the issues that they place on the table or which they mutually agree to discuss. (In our work we consult with groups that meet together in one location. Some consultants work with groups that teleconference; however, we do not do this.) One group could be the management team, the board of directors, or members of an organization which, therefore, has had an existence prior to the meeting and has a history of working together as a group (referred to as a *cousins group* in the old sensitivity training and t-group experiences). Another group may be representatives of city and county governments, development organizations, merchants associations, clean and beautiful groups, members of local labor unions, and representatives of different segments of the community. These people assemble for the first time as a group, know one another to varying degrees, and have never worked together before as a unit. This group would be referred to as a "strangers group" by the sensitivity and t-group trainers and as a zero-history group by Fisher and Ellis (1990).

Community

The people, organizations, and institutions that reside in a particular area and that create the environment within which they work, play, and live. We do not mean to imply that this must be a city or town or that the members would be found only within the legal boundaries of an incorporated government. We also think of a community of people with a common interest. So, for example, we may work with representatives of the community of environmentalists as they address an issue or the community of engineers, officials, and other interested parties in solid waste management.

Problem Solving

A multistep process in which an individual or group identifies that a problem exists, defines the problem, generates solutions to the problem, evaluates the solutions, chooses a solution or solutions, agrees to the implementation of the solution, and addresses the evaluation of the solution and implementation. A group or individual may engage in any or all of these particular steps in a process. All of these steps add up to problem solving. Note that frequently an emphasis is placed on creativity in this process. We treat the creativity aspect as implicit.

Decision Making

We use it as almost a synonym for problem solving. While some in the academic fields that study decision making speak of decision making as the simple act of making a choice among several alternatives, we treat it as the broader process of defining problems, inventing solutions, choosing an option, and working through issues of implementation.

Group Processes

The procedures and operations by which a group functions. They may be consciously selected and then rigorously adhered to by the group or they may be unconsciously opted for by a group. Group processes come in a wide variety of shapes and sizes, ranging from Robert's Rules of Order to unstructured and leaderless groups to highly structured systems for constraining interaction and everything in between. One of the responsibilities of a facilitator is to help the group use an appropriate and optimal group process.

Break-out Groups, Small Groups, and Large Groups

The different groups used during an intensive working session with a client group. Some activities are accomplished with the entire client group assembled in plenary session and acting as a large group. This may be 30 people sitting together around a horseshoe arrangement of tables. In order to efficiently address several issues the client group members are often assigned into several small or break-out groups. In these break-out sessions, the small groups typically comprise as few as 5 or as many as 10 people. In the break-out session the groups are assigned a specific task or set of tasks, such as brainstorming ideas about how to resolve a problem.

Intensive Working Sessions

Times for groups to work that are normally scheduled within a 1- to 3-day block of time and typically occur at a site removed from the normal, day-to-day operations of the group. The intense work within a compressed time frame allows the group to focus its attentions to the task. Some clients call these sessions *retreats*. They use that term not in the sense of running away from a bad situation but as a group withdrawal for purposes of study, meditation, and reflection. Other clients and colleagues feel that *retreat* is too negative a term and call them *advances*. Whatever the client or colleague calls them, the group work sessions are best scheduled as intensive and extended blocks of time away from the home location.

FRAMEWORK FOR THE BOOK

This book is presented in three parts. These three parts refer specifically to what a facilitator of community and decision-making groups does before, during, and after a facilitated session. Part I addresses what a facilitator should do before the actual facilitated work session with the client group. Part II, the during portion, deals with what the facilitator should be doing while the facilitated session is under way. Part III speaks to the time after the session, and concerns completing the project, generating the report, and the follow-up. These divisions have evolved for us as we worked with participants in our training sessions and helped them to better conceptualize what is involved in facilitation work. These delimitations are used in this book to help structure our thinking and your learning. It should be recognized that a facilitator attempts to look at a project holistically, by keeping in mind all of the concerns during all phases of working with clients.

Before

Considerable preparation is necessary *before* the facilitated session begins. Because of the nature of public service work at a major university, because our organization has conducted several high profile facilitation projects, and because of the reputation individual faculty members have developed as facilitators, we are often asked to facilitate groups. Requests are received by phone, mail, and fax and by referral from other agencies. We screen these requests to determine if the group really needs a facilitator or just thinks it does. Part of the screening process is to talk with an individual (group contact person) and assess from him or her:

- what is the purpose of the meeting;
- who will be attending the meeting; and
- why a facilitator appears to be needed?

In this discussion we will inform the contact person of what we do and do not do as facilitators. We also present our views about when we feel it is appropriate for a group to use a facilitator and when we believe a leader, expert, or manager is needed to keep the group on track. We believe facilitators can be effective when the group wants to:

- achieve consensus about a decision or plan of action;
- use a structured process to focus the group's energy and emotions;
- involve multiple agencies and community groups in discussion and decision making about an emotional issue or a common agenda;
- include the chairperson as a contributor of content in the discussion and debate;
- utilize expert information in the decision-making process (this requires special rules and procedures if the expert is not to overwhelm the group);
- produce an action plan for work assignments and project responsibilities; or
- engage in a problem-solving process to discover creative solutions.

Facilitators attempt to create an optimal design for a group process to meet the client's needs and respect the group as an entity. There is a range of possible designs and the intent is to find an appropriate one that serves the client and meets professional standards. The facilitator educates the clients by making them aware of the possibilities and moving the clients to a better understanding of group problem solving.

The need for a facilitator, the conditions under which facilitated meetings best function, clarifying the needs of the *client* group, desired outcomes and strategies, and arrangements for interviewing participants are further discussed in what we call the *design dance*. Sometimes the dance includes several meetings, phone calls, visits to the community, and negotiating visits to the meeting facility to arrange for accommodations. Once these arrangements are made we confirm them in a letter of agreement or contract with the client group specifying what we think we have agreed to do and what we expect the client group to do and when. In some instances the letter of agreement is modified to more clearly indicate what is going to happen, when, for whom, and at what costs. Sometimes, especially when the work is with a repeat customer, the dance is abbreviated and only a verbal agreement is made.

During

This part of the book deals with the obvious steps in the process of working with a community group or client. These are the activities that easily come to mind when one contemplates facilitating a group. It is the "hot" and "sexy" phase and the one that new facilitators tend to fret about the most. It is our contention that the *during* phase is only one of three parts and that all three must be considered and attended to with care. In fact, if you have not properly attended to the beginning phase and you have not reconciled important issues around your role and what is expected, you have created an untenable situation for yourself. Not taking care of the design dance means that the during part will be more demanding on you, will be more frustrating for the group, and may have set the group and yourself up for failure.

What happens from when the meeting *starts* until it is *completed* is the subject of the part of the book about "during the facilitated meeting itself." Managing the process and facilitating the meeting includes such things as:

- starting the meeting to break the ice and set the process in motion,
- involving participants in discussing their expectations,
- drawing the agenda items from participants,

- working on agenda items,
- checking in with participants to see if the facilitator and the group are on the right track,
- working toward consensus,
- managing dominant personalities and members who have hidden agendas,
- organizing information to make decisions,
- specifying needed actions,
- gaining commitment to action and designating responsibilities, and
- closing the meeting.

We like to close each meeting with a discussion of actions and responsibilities (see Friend & Hickling, 1987, for their discussion of commitment packages). Who will take responsibility for mailing out a newsletter about this group's plans and project assignments? Ideally, we also like to put these actions into a time frame:

- What will you do this evening after the meeting to begin work on your responsibility/the groups action plan?
- What will you do Monday to work on your action/responsibilities?
- When can you complete all of your responsibilities?
- When should the facilitator or someone else come back and meet with the group to review accomplishments and develop a new action plan?
- What are the first steps that need to be taken?
- Who is/are the policy champions(s) for this?

After

The *after* part is concerned with what follows the end of the meeting. So this part of the book addresses how the facilitator tries to wrap up his or her direct involvement and how to hand off the task to the group to ensure carry through and continuity. The whole facilitation process is one that tries to build a sense of ownership so that the meeting ends with commitment on the part of the whole group, or at least a significant number of individuals in the group, to carry forward the work that has been discussed. The goal of facilitated group problem solving should be to leave the group members with the potential to act on their own.

Facilitators normally leave the group or town after the meeting ends. The after part is concerned with the transition from facilitator assistance to the group working on its own. Questions that ought to be addressed by the facilitator include:

- What has the facilitator left with the group to empower it to organize its resources and take action?
- Does the group have enough information to do one thing immediately after the close of the meeting to begin achieving its goals?
- What can individuals do on the next Monday morning to begin achieving their goals?

After discussions are held in the context of what was specified in the action plan from the during part of the meeting. When working on a facilitation contract with a client, we typically offer to work with the group in a day-long or a half-day follow-up session some number of months after the facilitated work session. We come back to the group to review its actions and deviations from the plan. It is the group's plan, so we are not in the role of policing its progress, but we help by asking:

- Why did some parts of the action plan get implemented while others did not?
- Was there a problem of inadequate resources and how might that be overcome?
- Why were some things added and other things deleted from the plans? Were there compelling reasons for these changes? Did the entire group or community have an opportunity to participate in making the changes?
- How will you maintain support for your efforts?

The follow-up visit is one attempt to have the group take time to evaluate its progress and see if there is a need to restructure its plan. Have group members accomplished more than they realize and do they need to consider new directions and goals for their community? Also, it is an opportunity for the group to recognize and reward its efforts.

PART I

The Before Phase
or the Design Dance

As facilitators with community groups as clients, we assist in determining exactly what the clients' interests are, what they think the problem seems to be, what the issues really are (as seen from a more objective outside view), what they hope to accomplish, and what they must accomplish. This is done in order to determine whether facilitation services are even appropriate to their task and precisely what set of facilitation services would be the best fit to their needs. This process of initiating contact with potential clients and establishing what to do for them is one in which there are many variations and no one right approach. The same consultant will go through different approaches with different clients, depending on the circumstances of the client and the consultant at that particular time.

This phase, which we refer to as the before phase (because it is before the actual facilitated meeting or work session), is seen by us as a *design dance*. As the consultant who is offering a set of facilitation services to the community group client we attempt to *lead* while the client follows. The beat of the music is determined by the client and the client's time frame. The particular dance steps follow a pattern but can be improvised upon to endless variation. Occasionally, the dance is a bizarre event choreographed to accompany a symphony fantastique. On other occasions it is a mild and restrained box step, a lambada, or a break dance. No matter what the particulars are, it is a dance because the two partners engage in a mutually reactive set of steps, progress in a roundabout manner across the dance floor, and move on to other and bigger things from that one dance or part company after a dance that fails to entice.

The three chapters in this part discuss the full aspect of the design phase. Chapter 1 looks at the initiation of the dance and the acquisition of information on which to base design decisions. Chapter 2 presents the core design issues that need to be resolved. Finally, Chapter 3 discusses the physical layout of the meeting space and some other physical issues.

CHAPTER 1

Initiating the Design Dance

The focus of attention during the design dance should be on the creation of a plan for a group session that has the best chance for meeting the needs of the client. What is involved then is discovering what the client wants and needs and trying to match that with a meeting design and set of techniques. Sometimes this involves educating the client about what is possible, desirable, and optimal. Sometimes this is a process that results in the discovery or invention of new ways of doing things as the facilitator reaches beyond the tried and true to better serve a client. In every case the facilitator works with the client to establish a definition and mutual understanding regrading the preparation for the meeting.

A LONG, WILD, AND CRAZY DESIGN DANCE

We received a call from the chair of a county commission seeking our services to work with an ad hoc committee that would comprise citizens and public officials. The request initially was to replicate a community-wide strategic planning process that we had performed for some other counties in the state. The initial phone conversation was the first screening device. The first phone call is an opportunity to gain some information and come to a quick determination as to whether this appears to be a go or a no-go situation. The initial conversation may reveal that the potential client is looking for an expert to evaluate its operations or to provide an expert opinion or solution. At times such a service is exactly what the client needs and, if this is evident, the client ought to be steered to a provider of such services. In this example the conversation with the commission chair revealed that he understood the difference between an expert-consultant and a facilitator and was in fact looking for a facilitator for the committee.

A meeting was arranged for several of the commissioners, some of their staff, and us to sit down and discuss the issue at hand and to allow us to gather information so as to design an appropriate process and submit a short proposal for services. At that meeting a strange dance unfolded. As the discussion developed, it became clear that a newly elected county commission chair was seeking input regrading the development of the county and growth management issues from a committee or task force of citizens and some appointed officials. We, as the consultants, discussed what we had done in some similar situations in the state for other counties that were attempting to deal with similar situations. We offered a draft sample contract proposal (see Appendix A) that outlined what we might do and the possible range of prices based upon our projects with other counties. We stressed two things. First, we stressed that this ought to be a project that would be supported by the county, the city, and the Chamber of Commerce, and that we would prefer to sign a contract with all those parties rather than just the county government. Second, we stressed that the committee should look at growth management or community strategic planning. The commission chair said to us, "Right. I know what you mean . . . land use planning!" We said no, not land use planning as the focus for the group's work but broadly looking at development and management of growth and development, which is much more than land use planning. He said, "Yeah, land use planning." We said that we saw land use planning as a tool to achieving what we were discussing but not the entire ball of wax. He said, "Land use planning!!!!" We managed to point the county commissioners in the direction of a state agency responsible for community affairs for particular advice on land use planning and suggested that they might want to work closely with their regional council of governments on such a project.

Walking out of the meeting, we were convinced that this was a project we did not want to pursue. We could not get over our failure to communicate. The dance had seemed to us to be a nonstarter or one in which we had been hearing different tunes and could not get off to anything. We chalked that one up to a learning experience and got out of there gladly.

Roughly 2 months later we received a call from the leaders of the task force that had been appointed by the county commission asking us to come and explain our proposal to a meeting of the task force's executive committee. Our reaction was basically one of shock. Over the phone we attempted to convey that our proposal was different from what the task force seemed to want and that we did not believe our proposal was a viable alternative. After repeated requests we agreed to meet with the task force's executive committee.

At that meeting we were able to explain what we had envisioned and had done in other counties and how that differed from what they were up to. We did our best to explain that our facilitation services and project design were not appropriate for what they had in mind. We attempted to put them off and steer them to some other organization. The meeting concluded with some frustration on both parts. The executive committee was feeling at a loss to get going on the task force assignment, to review and recommend a new land use plan, but did not know how to proceed. We felt frustrated because we thought that there was no match between our services and what they wanted and because we wanted to escape from a hopeless situation.

We were invited to another meeting of the executive committee. We were specifically asked to lay out a process that the task force could use that would have us serving as facilitators. It was made clear that the task force was not responsible for developing a new land use plan but was to suggest changes and policies to guide a new land use plan. We again tried to explain the value, from our point of view, of having the group look at a broader range of issues related to community-wide strategic planning. Furthermore, we explained our lack of experience in assisting a group dealing only with land use planning. The committee members made clear that it was only land use planning that was on the table and that our assistance was desired for that task. We agreed to attend a subsequent meeting of the executive committee with a proposal for the project as envisioned.

We put together a proposal for a process centered around an intensive 2-day-work session. At that session the task force members would come to a series of assessments of the faults and positive aspects of the existing land use plan. They would suggest the changes and enhancements for the new plan and the policies that should guide the development of a new plan. The work session would be scheduled for a few months later so that the task force's subcommittees could work on portions of the plan. At the meeting the executive committee looked over the new draft proposal and asked pointed questions. Specifically, they indicated that the total cost was prohibitive relative to the resources available. We pointed out why an intensive two-day working session away from the community was so productive and positive. They objected to the cost of such a session (such as lodging, meals, our services). We suggested a range of other possibilities and specified that one option we would not consider was a long series of 1 or 1 1/ 2-hour meetings. After considerable discussion we arrived at an agreement to redraft a process that would consist of a series of eight 4-hour meetings starting in the new calendar year and scheduled over 4 to 5 months. The process would have subcommittees review elements of the plan and report at a meeting on their findings and suggestions to the full task force. The full task force would then deliberate and arrive at conclusions. We would conduct the meetings, provide advice to the subcommittees, attend executive committee meetings, and serve as recorders and reporters of the large task force meetings. We argued for a general description of the process that would be used at each meeting and for decision making by consensus.

The proposal was revised along the lines discussed above. The proposal was presented to the full task force at one of its meetings. A time for questions and answers was included. A few concerns that were raised led to some minor adjustments. At the next meeting of the task force the full membership concurred that the task force, acting for the county, should enter into the contract. We did so with the chair of the task force signing the contract. It should be pointed out that we still had some qualms about this particular project and had consistently stated that we were not serving as expert consultants on land use planning.

Without going into a full account of the task force, allow us to say that the work of the task force went quite well. Almost all of the meetings were well attended. The subcommittees engaged in good reviews and contributed to the full review of the land use plan. The task force easily developed a reliance upon consensual decision making. Only on one controversial subject did the task force consider voting with a majority rule to arrive at a decision, but the task force members indicated that a vote would not be acceptable and continued to talk until consensus was achieved.

After each meeting we assembled a written record of accomplishments and agreements. At the next meeting the task force approved its work to date and clarified our record, fixing errors, and suggesting improvements. As time went on the task force saw its report to the county evolve. The process worked well and a set of policies emerged that was generally acceptable to the county population and was used for the development of new land use plans.

So, the moral of this example is that the facilitator needs to be patient and open. The facilitator must be open and receptive to where the dance will lead, who will take the lead, and when the lead will change. The facilitator must not close out the possibility for something good to result from the design dance. The facilitator must not get locked into only one way of thinking and attempt to write off other ideas as irrelevant. The facilitator must leave his or her ego at the door during design meetings, as well as during an actual facilitated session. That is to say facilitators must not delude themselves into thinking that only they have the correct answer or a monopoly on the truth. So, stay humble, go with the flow of the design dance, see where it leads, and remain open to possibilities.

ACQUIRING INFORMATION
FOR DESIGN DECISIONS

Before you can begin designing a group process to suit the client and the client's task you must obtain some information so that your choices can be made as intelligently as possible. In this regard, there are two primary things that you should find out. First, determine exactly who your client is. Second, gather information about the problem, issue, or the decision that the client is trying to make, that is, the purpose.

Finding Out Who Your Client Is

It is very easy to get confused about who you are working for. We know that this is true because we do it from time to time. Do not confuse the contact individual or the steering committee with your client. Remain open to who your client really is! We were contacted by a superintendent of schools to do some planning work with the board. From the contacts we had and the way that the superintendent talked it was clear to us that he was our client or that the school system as a corporate entity was our client and that he personified the school system. Even during the interviews of the board members, this notion of who our client was stayed the same. Only at the beginning of the group's work session did it become shockingly clear to us that our client was the school board itself. We were there only because the school board wanted it and insisted on it. The board members did not want the superintendent at the meeting beyond the first five minutes and believed that the superintendent was part of the problem. Once we understood all this we were able to come to terms with what we had to do. And that was to serve the group, the school board members, in its deliberations and discussions.

When you work with a management team of a community organization you can run into the other trap. With the school system we erred in thinking that the executive officer, the superintendent, was the client. With the managers of an existing organization or with the board of an agency or authority it is very easy to assume that you are working for the team. They may use that language and lots of sports analogies to maintain the notion of a management team. Beware! Be careful! Sometimes the board members know and the employees know that it is all a smoke screen and controlled image. Your client is really an autocratic executive officer who merely talks team play and participation. When you get to the group session you find that no participants want to open up and be creative until they know what the executive director already plans to do. What do you do at that point? Think about how to avoid getting in that position again.

Be clear about finding out who you are really working for. Do not just assume that the person who writes the check is the client; this person may only be the officer acting on instructions for the real client. Nothing can guarantee that you do not make this mistake. After all you are only human. What you can do is attend to the design dance with as much concentration as possible. You can also gather as much information ahead of time as you and the client can afford to have you do.

Information Gathering

If you are going to design a process to meet the client's needs, and even more important, to serve the client's real interests as you understand them, you should collect information during the before phase so you can customize the group work session and the process for the session so that it is appropriate. This means that you will engage in interviewing or survey work or group interviews or premeetings or some combination of these. We like to do as much information gathering as we can and with an agreement to share as little of that information with the group as possible. We prefer not to share a lot of information because it makes for deadly boring beginnings and we prefer to have the group members publicly share such information among themselves. The information collected is meant to be used primarily in making decisions about the meeting design and process. Admittedly, there are times when due to constraints it is not possible to collect much information before the group's work session.

In the best of all worlds you would be able to speak privately and off-the-record with each person who will attend the session. You will also be able to administer some form of a questionnaire. These would give you both contextually rich open-ended responses to key questions and a set of easily analyzed closed-ended responses. Finally, in this best of all possible worlds, you would have a meeting prior to the actual group work session, possibly over breakfast or lunch, when you could build some common expectations about the group session, find out what questions and concerns there are, and hear about necessary last minute adjustments. Alas and alack (with an accompanying wringing of one's hands), rarely does this best of all worlds exist; and when it does it is but for a fleeting moment. Years ago, before the budget crunches caught up with us and when our work load was not as heavy, we were able to do the above on most of our projects. Now we must make do with less.

So realistically, what can you do? How can you comfortably make do with less? As a rule, more is better than less. If you cannot afford to interview everyone who will attend the session, then do whatever you can manage. Try to talk to more than just one contact person if at all possible. If you rely on only one person you never know if you are being sold a bill of goods. It may be that this person is trying to gain control of the group and has decided to bring you in as leverage. One of us had exactly this happen to him. He was asked in to facilitate a meeting and when he got there found that the chairperson was planning on running the meeting, the group members were not expecting a facilitator, and one person had suckered him in. WHOOPS! As a facilitator you must keep your eyes open, understand organization behavior, and be honest with yourself that you are only human, therefore, you will occasionally err.

Two specific cautions can be offered. The first caution is that you should not acquire information only from the formal leadership of a group or organization. You should attempt to speak with a sample of the group, including some of the informal leaders if possible. If you attempt to speak with only a sampling of the participants, you can ask each person to recommend one or two other people with whom you should speak. This may help identify a few group members who are key, not based upon their formal organizational positions, because of their knowledge, status, power, or whatever. Obviously, this will help to provide a wider insight and different views. The second caution deals with reality and perceptions. Our rational-scientific culture puts a premium on discovering reality. It values that hard-edged reality. It is very easy to want to discover the reality of the client's situation. You need to remember that perceptions and differences in perceptions of reality are often crucial. We do not want to engage in a philosophical argument of reality versus perceptions or whether reality exists separate from the act of perception. Quite simply, people act on what they perceive, hence their perceptions are important. Often a major problem in a group is that people perceive different problems (often in terms of their differing preferred solutions) and an important part of the group session will be sharing those perceptions and creating a commonly accepted version. So, talk to several people and encourage them to share with you their perceptions.

Efficient ways to gather information can be substituted for one-on-one interviews. You will have to give up the privacy of an interview and the ability to change questions based on responses. Various survey forms can be distributed to gather information. They might ask people to rate aspects of their community. Forms might ask people to generate short lists of issues that need to be addressed. Premeetings can be used to disseminate information about the group session and also to gather information from attendees. As part of a series of facilitated group problem-solving sessions for economic development in rural counties, premeetings were held to clarify the intent of the project, verify that the county wanted to participate, and collect some initial sense of the opportunities and problems that the county faced. At the premeeting for each county, cards and marker pens were given to the participants and they were asked to write down an asset and a challenge for economic development in their county. People were told to write one asset or one challenge per card. These cards were then passed around so the participants could see the ideas that had been generated without knowing who had generated them. They were given the opportunity to complete another card or two if they thought of something else that had not been written down or if an idea on a card had generated a new idea (piggy-backing). Such techniques enable the consultant to efficiently collect information and engage in conceptual planning for the group's problem-solving session. Generally, the premeeting allows for information gathering and also allows the facilitator to allay people's concerns and clarify what will be expected of them at the intensive group work session.

A mentor (before we ever talked so much about such things) once said to us as we went to interview participants before finishing the design phase, "As you listen to these people, remember to believe no **one** but believe **everyone.**" It is important to remember that no one individual has a monopoly on the truth. Each person will see reality from his or her particular perspective and set of biases. You need to listen to everyone and not allow yourself to get sucked into a single individual's views and opinions. Listen to it all and realize that as an outsider you may come to a better understanding of their reality than they have themselves.

SUMMARY

Please do not be disappointed if your own design dances prove to be somewhat less dramatic than the long example that is discussed in this chapter. It is not always a case of the client wanting to waltz while you try to limbo, but it can happen. Make sure that you talk it through with the client and groups with which you will work. Collect the information and then try to discover a design that might work to meet their needs. Recognize that there is probably not just one optimal design that you must discover, but a multiplicity of designs that might work well. Your job is to engage in a fruitful dance and acquire the information so that you can find one of these that matches up well with the client's needs.

CHAPTER 2

Issues to Consider in the Design Dance

As the facilitators gather information and interact with the client several issues must be faced and smaller design decisions must be made. Some of these issues place the facilitator in the role of educator. Herein the facilitator educates the client about group dynamics, what can and cannot be done with groups, and so on. While the facilitator is not an expert about sewerage treatment or downtown revitalization, the facilitator is an expert about group process. The facilitator uses this expertise to design the best process possible and to raise the knowledge of the client.

DEALING WITH NAIVE EXPECTATIONS ABOUT WHAT CAN BE DONE

With a client new to facilitation or one with only limited experience, there is often a naive set of beliefs about what can be done in a facilitated meeting. These naive expectations are usually at the two extremes. At one extreme some clients do not understand how a meeting that is facilitated by an outside consultant can or will be different from their usual sort of meeting. On the other hand are clients who expect too much; they are looking for a facilitator to run a 4-hour session in which 20 people are to write a mission statement, brainstorm goals, set goals, establish priorities for the goals, and devise a work program for the coming year.

In dealing with both extremes you attempt to clarify what can realistically be expected to happen. For the doubters the best approaches seem to be showing them the results of other sessions.

Sometimes we cynically believe that the best use of reports is to demonstrate to other clients what someone else has done. Instead of presenting reports, a client can be referred to previous clients to hear their testimonials. If you have no track record to offer a client, all you can do is patiently explain what your role is and how what you do frees up the group to concentrate on its tasks.

For the over eager clients who think that eight months of work can be crammed into a 4-hour session you must lower the expectations to a manageable level. Tell them that you cannot get that done in a 4-hour session. Tell them that you do not expect to be able to generate goals, refine the list, and set priorities among goals in four hours, let alone do everything else.

The facilitator is the party with the knowledge and expertise about group process as opposed to the topic or content that the client group will address. It has to be the responsibility of the facilitator to engage in some reality therapy with the client or planning committee about what can and cannot be done in the scheduled group work session.

SELLING THE NOTION OF INTENSIVE GROUP WORK SESSIONS

Clients, especially new clients, have a hard time believing that an intensive group work session is worth the money and effort. The client will indicate that overnight lodging is too expensive, that a series of weekly 2-hour meetings would be sufficient to get the work done, that going away is too great a sacrifice to make, and that a conference room in some building in town may not be all that great but will serve as a good meeting space.

Taking a group away, out of town or at least out of the office building, for a solid and extended block of time is the best thing that you can do for the group. Psychologically, it seems to break people out of the usual ways of thinking and to say that we are in a new place to do some new thinking. Logistically, once participants are at the meeting location they are there and will not be running back to their offices to make quick phone calls (and not returning for hours). If the meeting is in their usual place of work they will treat the session as no different from their regular work, so phone calls will interrupt, emergencies and crises will be taken care of, meetings will start late and end early.

Facilitated sessions can be done in less than 1-day units. Facilitated sessions can be done right there in town and in their buildings. You just need to be clear with the client about the not so obvious downside of staying in town or in the office (the downside of going away to a conference center are obvious to them). Fairly recently for some county level coalitions on children and youth we have had to devise as inexpensive a work session as we can—recognizing their very limited budgets and truly worthy missions and our own curtailed financial situation due to budget constraints. We arranged a meeting for them that ran 5 hours one afternoon (from 1:00 to 6:00) and then 4 hours the next morning (from 8:00 until noon) in a conference room or meeting space in their town but away from their usual offices. This allowed them to forego the expense of overnight lodging and meals but still creates a solid block of time to address their issues.

Our experience has been that more can be accomplished in a 2-day work session (roughly 14 to 18 hours of actual work time) than can be accomplished by a group in 30 or 40 1-hour meetings that are strung out over many months. The intense time frame allows a group to focus on the task, build a common understanding, not be distracted, and forge through to a final resolve about what to do and how to do it. If you must compromise, give up going out of town and try your best to get them to agree to scheduling meetings for long and solid blocks of time as opposed to 1- or 2-hour sessions over many weeks. The solid blocks of time for a group session allows the group to build momentum, stay intensely focused on the topic, and lose less time in getting started and concluding at sessions.

SPECIAL CONSIDERATIONS
WITH ZERO-HISTORY GROUPS

Working with groups that have no previous history presents special challenges. A big part of this is in working with the client to decide who the client is and who will attend the work session.

Often our zero-history groups are ones that are brought together to address community-wide issues and discuss economic development or strategic planning for the community. The special thing to be worked out with such groups, and that preexisting groups generally don't need to address, is the composition of the group. Exactly how many will attend is crucial information so that you can plan how large a team of facilitators to put together and what techniques might be best. Attending to the composition ensures that there will be sufficient diversity to represent the different interests and to enliven debate. Diversity of membership helps ensure that there will be requisite variety within the group to match the needs of the task (Ashby, 1958).

Diversity in Group Composition

With a zero-history group, the initial point of contact might be the executive director of a chamber of commerce or a development authority. We will meet with representatives of the initiating organization and talk about who else ought to be a part of the project if it is to really make a difference. The county government and the cities and school board members also become obvious candidates to include, as do the merchants' associations and downtown groups. Frequently further prodding on our part is necessary to get the group to consider other groups, who might not obviously be thought of as part of the issue arena. We will often ask pointed and painful questions such as, "Are there women who live in the community or are there only men?" or "Are there any ethnic or racial minorities that ought to be included?" The group members' eyes will flutter and then they will begin to think about a more broadly representative group. Further questioning will help the group to remember that there are a variety of groups and interests who are members of the community who also have a stake in economic development or strategic planning.

Our goal is to help to ensure that the initial contact group or steering committee does not automatically round up the usual suspects and that we do not end up with a "BOWGSAT" or "bunch of white guys sitting around a table." We will help the group to make the attempt to diversify itself and to better represent the many facets of the community. The facets that are left out differ from community to community. In some places it might be the Hispanic groups that you will have to remind them to include. In other places you might have to ask about the inclusion of representatives of organized labor. We believe that for community groups to think widely and creatively about issues they need to be as broadly representative and diverse as possible.

HETEROGENEOUS GROUPS

We strongly believe in the value of heterogeneous groups when working with community groups and most decision groups, whether they be zero-history groups or not. We believe that different points of view should be brought to the table in the group and in break-out groups. Having the diverse opinions gathered together allows everyone to hear these varying beliefs. The group processes employed will allow the group to recognize and value the differences and work to uncover common ground and mutually acceptable positions. Our belief is that diversity of group composition helps to enrich the process, spark creativity, better define problems, and ensure that the group does not complacently ignore some point of view (Ashby, 1958).

On one occasion we were asked by a county to consider submitting a proposal to facilitate a rather large scale project that involved multiple parties (homeowners, developers, environmentalists, and home builders) reviewing infrastructure development plans. The county asked several different consultants to consider submitting proposals. Typically, as university-based public service faculty, we try to avoid getting into competition with private sector consultants, so there was already a strike against the project. What tipped the balance against the project for us was that the county asked us to indicate what we would charge to execute the proposal exactly as their request for proposals laid it out. We indicated that we believed their proposal was flawed because it called for homogeneous small groups to work initially and then for consensus to be built across the small groups. We indicated that we thought it was a mistake to have only homeowners in some groups and only developers in others and so on. We thought that it would be problematic to try later to build consensus across such groups. When we were told that the project design was set and would not be changed, we decided that we would not submit a proposal. We later heard that the project encountered difficulties in trying to bridge the positions that had developed within the homogeneous groups. We believe that it is important for the facilitator to say no when he or she believes that the design is flawed or that the process will not respect the group.

Furthermore, as a steering committee begins to identify a list of possible members and someone on the steering committee says that a particular individual is a troublemaker or will complain about what the group does, we will indicate that the person ought to be included in the group. It is better to include such a person in the initial meetings so that he or she can bring additional perspectives to the group rather than excluding the troublemaker who may sabotage the group's plan. A more sinister view would be to involve these people so that they can be co-opted into being supporters of the project.

Obviously, when our contract is to work with only a management team or the board of an organization we do not demand that they hire or appoint new and diverse members. However, as a facilitator you can help a group to consider bringing in significant outsiders, such as key clients or constituents, to enrich the deliberations. The inclusion of stakeholders and others who are outside of the normal organization boundaries can help add diversity to the discussions and question some assumptions.

GROUP SIZE AND DESIGN FOR PROCESS

The counterbalancing force to greater diversity and representativeness is trying to keep the size of the group manageable. Obviously, the smaller the group due to whatever reasons, the harder it will be for the group to be widely diverse and representative. How large a group can be brought together and how large a group can the client afford to bring together? How large a group can we be expected to facilitate? There are no firm rules about this. Generally speaking, a group loses it smallness as the number of participants rises above ten. The old "magic number" seven plus or minus two is at work here. A good small group size is between five and nine. This allows for a diversity of viewpoints, does not allow for two people to gang up on one, and still keeps the number of person-to-person communication channels to a manageable number. The group can be seated in proximity around tables or in a circle of chairs.

As the number rises above 10 it becomes more and more unwieldy and requires greater attention to structuring the process and managing how the group operates. As it gets larger still the group loses its feelings of intimacy and begins to take on aspects of a public forum. In our experience another cutting point is reached at about 25 to 30 participants. It is still possible to design a meeting room and a process that allows 25 to 30 people to sit together, engage in some common work, and move toward consensus. With this large a number it becomes necessary to break them out into small groups for discussion and to accomplish subtasks for the overall process. Careful attention must be given to managing small group assignments and trying to ensure that the small group experience is additive to the overall flow. The graphical presentation of a typical design for a facilitated community group session for about 25 to 30 participants in Figure 2.1 shows the use of large and small group sessions.

Questions arise in cost of operation of a meeting or group work session because the number of facilitators that would be required has risen. Facilitators for each of the three or four groups would now have to be paid by the client. An overall master of ceremonies or grand facilitator or *games operations director* (that is GOD for short) may be necessary to run the whole show. If recorders (recording secretaries) are needed, as well as computer operators, the number of necessary bodies quickly increases. In fact we have done some projects where we have had 10 staff working on the project for 30 members in the client group. Such intense staffing is only possible when the cost of the

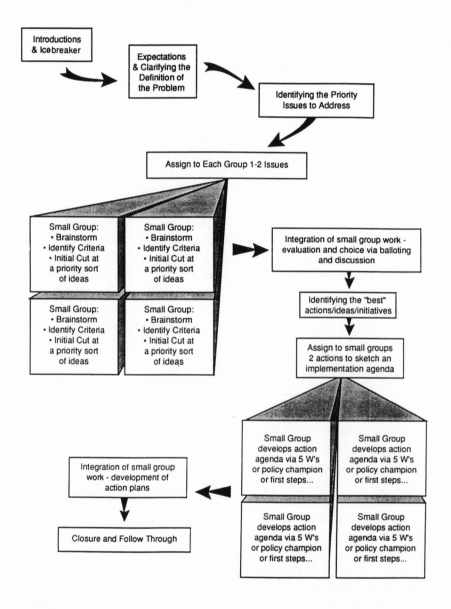

FIGURE 2.1 *Design for a typical facilitated community group session*

service to the client can be heavily subsidized. A 25-member client group can be run by as few as 3 facilitator team members but the facilitators will be exhausted by the end of the session. Furthermore, the small group facilitators will have to coordinate and follow similar procedures, in fact asking the same *cuing* questions, to ensure that there is compatibility between the small group products.

As you increase the size of the group beyond 30 you need to be very creative. You will have to either design a highly structured process for manipulating and controlling the group interaction and process, or you will have to loosen your control and believe that some chaos is a good thing. Highly structuring the process for very large groups to minimize interpersonal interaction is reflected in such techniques as Crawford Slip Writing technique (see VanGundy, 1988). On the extreme, such techniques show one approach for working with very large groups. To our way of thinking these very large gatherings have become assemblages that should not properly even be called groups anymore.

With two different groups that ranged well above the 30 as an upper limit number, we bought into creating some chaos and it worked quite well. Calling it chaos is an over statement, but with roughly 90 people in one client group and with approximately 140 in the other, things were rather crazy and run far more loosely while trying to maintain the large group and facilitated small group design that has worked well for us. The basic strategy was to train some of the client's members to serve as facilitators of small groups. In one of the very early design meetings for the group work session, the consultants floated this idea and got the steering committee thinking about who might act as small group facilitators. The steering committee was able to quickly identify a list of members who appeared to have the requisite abilities. A half-day session was scheduled prior to the group session at which the necessary number of people were run through a "quick and dirty" introduction to facilitation. The basic idea was presented and modeled for them. They were presented with a written script that they were to follow. (A generalized version of the script appears in Example 2.1)

Example 2.1   *Script for Small Group Facilitators*

1. *Introduction and Preliminary Stage*:

   Rationale: Allow for introduction and give some initial air time.

   Statement: "Take a minute and think of one word or a very short phrase that captures what you think is possible for our group *today* (or *next year* or in *five years*)."

   Process: Ask people to share their word or phrase and tell the group their name, what they do, and how long they have been a _____ group member.

2. *Explore the issue*:

   Rationale: Groups tend to be *solution minded*, that is, wanting to jump the gun to solutions, so first force a discussion of the problem.

   Statement: "Before we begin suggesting solutions or things that we would like to see done to address this issue, let's first make sure we understand the issue."

   Process: Ask people to think or write down what occurs to them about this issue—what it means to them, how it affects their work, and how it affects the community and this group. Then work the group in a round robin fashion (go to the first person and ask for one thing, then the next person, etc.) and write on newsprint what they say. Give them a chance to react to the *problem definition* before going to the next step.

3. *Generation of Ideas and Suggestions:*

   Rationale: Groups work best by first *brainstorming* and then evaluating the ideas, so we will first generate ideas and try to keep them from getting into evaluative discussion and criticizing what people suggest.

   Statement: "Please jot down on paper all those things that you can think of that might be done to deal with this issue—these might solve the issue, mitigate it, and so on. Please don't censor yourself, put down even wild ideas, things that don't seem easily implementable, etc. At this point we are not worrying about how to do or who will do these."

   Process: Again use a round robin for the individual members' ideas to the newsprint. Do *not* let them get into a critique of one another's ideas. Tell them that they should listen to the ideas but not get into an evaluation. Be sure to leave some room next to, or around, the items to make clarification or record the dollars.

4. *Review Ideas for Clarification*:

Rationale: Separates the discussion and consideration of what is intended from the initial generation and the judgment of the quality of the ideas.

Statement: "Before we try to rate the ideas to identify the very best or most imaginative new approaches, let's review these to make sure we understand what is meant. If it seems logical to the group to combine a couple of items as we go along, because they are duplicates or they combine to make a better whole, we will do that."

Process: Work down through the list asking if the idea is clear, are there questions, and so on. Do *not* let a debate go on between two or three individuals on the merits of the idea—tell them that we will use a technique to let them express their judgments of the quality of the ideas.

5. *Simple "Poll" to Identify the Best Ideas*:

Rationale: A vote or poll can limit the problems caused by status differential and domineering personalities and it can allow for a more efficient use of the time.

Statement: "Now, individually review the list and spend five dollars on the items you think are best. You can not break down a dollar into change, that is you must spend them as whole dollars. You should spend your money in the way that reflects your judgment of the quality of the suggestions. You can spend all five dollars on one item, four dollars on one and one dollar on another, etc."

Process: Go around the group and have each person tell you the items on which they spent their dollars. Keep a running tally of the dollars spent on the newsprint. Let them examine the result of the poll and discuss the outcome—does it make sense, give a chance for an impassioned plea for more votes, etc. If the group members feel they need a chance to vote again, let them do so. Once the group feels okay about the list, move on.

6. *Identifying the "Group's" Role and Activities Relative to the Top Rated Ideas*:

Rationale: Probably the greatest weakness of strategic planning is in moving to implementation. In order to begin to move to the decision making regarding how to implement and gear the organization to grapple with the issues, the group will be asked to discuss the role that this group should best play for each of the top suggested "solutions."

Statement: "Let's take each of the top rated solutions in turn and indicate in broad terms how the group could or should begin to work toward the accomplishment of that."

Process: Go through a controlled discussion of this for each item. If you feel the need use the structured approach of having participants individually think, then report in round robin, and so on. You will probably find at this point that they are able to focus their discussion with only mild guidance and control from you.

There was not sufficient time to allow them to role play at the short training session, but there was time for questions and answers. The folks left the training session with a sense that their task was manageable but they had some trepidations. The session for the large groups started with plenary sessions and then people were asked to break out into small groups. They streamed out all over the meeting facility as a large number of small groups got under way. The consultants were around to serve as problem resolvers and to manage the flow. In the group session of 140 people there was only one consultant. For the 90-person group there were three of us to resolve problems and to run the plenary sessions. We used the plenary sessions to hear reports from the small groups, as a time for folks to lobby one another about what they thought were the best ideas, and to vote. In the meeting for 140 people the plenary sessions were essentially introductions, reporting from the small groups, and wrap-up sessions.

The moral of it all is that the size of the group and the design of the meeting are wound up together. You can't design the right meeting without knowing the size of the group but the influence runs the other way as well.

CHOICE OF FACILITATION TEAM

Part of the design dilemma is trying to find a particular design that works for the clients, at a cost they can live with, and one that allows you not to have to do it all by yourself. There are times when working alone is the best way to go. If the group is a small management team that needs to work together on a problem set and an immediate written record is not essential, it may be best to go it alone with the group or at most involve one other person. If there are two of you working a group you can either specialize with one acting as facilitator and the other as recorder or computer operator. Some people like to facilitate and have another person act as the scribe (or recorder) on the flip charts and to hang the flip charts. Other folks like to work the group and write down the key phrases on the flip charts themselves. Determine how you will be comfortable in working with the other team members and what roles you can reasonably expect them to fulfill. Understand that just because someone is a good facilitator does not mean that person will be a good recorder.

As you work with larger groups you may need to assemble larger teams if you cannot rely on the participants to operate in unfacilitated small groups or to serve as their own small group moderators. The larger the team you put together the more time you will need to spend in supervisory and coordinating activities. You may need to bring along one person to act just as floater and coordinator. The facilitator in the large group sessions may not facilitate a small group but could float and observe how the small groups go. It may be necessary to have a facilitator and a recorder for each small group if you are trying to use an elaborate process or to build a "model" on a computer to aid the group in its work.

One important thing to remember is that if you design a meeting that your team will help conduct, you need to bring your whole team to the front of the room and introduce everyone as a full team member. If you stand at the front of the room and point to your colleagues at the back, you will be sending the message that you are important and they are less important or useful. If you introduce everyone together and say that you are a team it communicates greater equality among the team members and will allow you to flexibly play different roles, such as tag-team facilitation (just like tag-team wrestling). This is especially important if your team is of mixed gender. Be sure not to unconsciously send the message that a female colleague is just a secretary there to type.

The greatest benefit from working with a team is that there is another person for you to confer with about how the meeting is going or what you might try to do to get around an obstacle. If you are on you own you will not have the opportunity to step aside and talk things through with a colleague.

WHEN SHOULD YOU SAY NO?

Sometimes you should tell potential clients that you are unwilling to work with them or unwilling to proceed in the way that they ask. There are no easy rules to follow in this regard. You should be sensitive to your professional and ethical standards and be ready to stand by those if you believe that they would be compromised. For example, if you feel that the contact person is trying to use you as a tool to manipulate a group to arrive at a prearranged conclusion, you should be ready to say no to doing the meeting or to doing it in the way that the person wants. Or the group may be taking on a topic that you feel is morally or ethically wrong, and if your moral standards would keep you from serving effectively as a facilitator you should not attempt to do so.

Our experience has been that you should also say *no* if the group is addressing a topic about which you are an expert. One of our fundamental rules for a facilitator, mentioned earlier, is that you should "leave your ego at the door." This means that your ego is strong enough that you can put it aside and not let what the group does challenge it, but it also means that you will remain detached from the content of the discussion. If you believe that you are one of the primary experts in the topic that is under discussion or if a major part of your ego is defined by your professional attachment to the topic, you should say *no* to being the facilitator for this group. You will find that it is almost impossible for you to be neutral and work toward the group's objectives. You will want to speak to the subject, to correct what seem to you obvious errors and misunderstandings, and to sell your favorite ideas and solutions. When you start to do these things you will find that the group will treat you as a content expert and will not treat you as a facilitator; the group will not allow you to easily move back and forth between the roles. Our advice is to get someone else to serve as facilitator and for you to join the group as a technical expert by sitting at the table or along the wall as a resource person.

We also believe that you should say *no* when the client makes so many demands or last minute changes that compromise the facilitated process that has been designed. While you want to be flexible and adapt to changes to ensure a good session, you ought to draw the line when you feel that all the good has been squeezed out. For example, five of us attended a conference of a statewide business/development organization to facilitate five small break-out sessions scheduled to run for approximately 6 hours (a couple hours one afternoon and the following morning) that were to get the people involved as active participants in planning a part of the organization's work agenda. At the conference facility we were told that the afternoon would have to be used for another purpose and that the whole morning would still be for the planned purpose. Being flexible, we said okay. Late that evening we were told that some of the morning would have to be given to something else. The next morning we were told that even less time was available. We were now looking at having only an hour and one half. Well, the program ran late so that we really only had about 45 minutes. We went ahead and did it because the person on our team who was in charge wanted to establish a relationship with this organization. In our estimation we would have been better off saying no because the very small amount of time available did not permit anything productive to be accomplished. The moral here is that when in your opinion the group or process cannot *win*, you probably ought to say *no*.

Finally, we recognize that saying no to a potential client is not easy. It can be hard to do because it means that money and payment for services rendered will not be coming to you. It can be hard because you want to work with a client in order to build a rapport for other work that may later come your way. It can be hard because doing something for a client may give you entry into other markets in which you want to do business. It can be hard to say no for a variety of reasons. However, sometimes you need to say no, or to say no in a managed way. An option you should explore is saying no to one way of doing business by offering to say yes to another way of serving the client. You can say yes we will do this but . . . , and indicate that the time frame needs to change or that the group composition needs to be adjusted or whatever. You can engage in the full drama of the design dance and try to lead the client to a better scheme by saying no to what was requested and directing the design dance to what seems to be a better design.

LAST MINUTE CHANGES

Be flexible about what the topics of discussion are or will be. If you have completed preliminary interviews or other forms of data collection even as little as a week prior to the date of the group work session, you must keep in mind that other things can happen which drastically change the focus of the group or the topics considered crucial. For example, we had collected preliminary information from a group of people from a county that planned to meet to discuss recreation issues. The preliminary conversations revealed concerns about lack of park space, inadequate sports programming, inadequate active recreation programming, and desires for protecting and buffering a scenic and wild river that flowed through the county. The day before the group session the commissioner of the state environmental and natural resources department announced that in an effort to save funds, the state park located in the county would be closed within two weeks. The meeting went off as scheduled, but the initial topic of conversation was obviously very different from what we had planned. The group spent the first couple hours talking about and complaining about the state agency action. We turned the discussion to addressing the question of what could the county residents do to influence decision making about state park closures being made in the capitol. When the group members felt that they had identified a local response plan that made sense, they wanted to proceed with the previously discussed subject matter, that is, their local recreation program. As a facilitator you must be ready, willing, and eager to go with the group in the direction that is salient and crucial to them, that is, to let go of your plans and thoughts about what is important and be responsive to the group.

The recreation group example discussed above is not our only instance in which we have changed our plans to be responsive to the group. The whole reason for data collecting and interviewing prior to the group session is so that you can plan a custom-designed process that will be likely to help the group get through its work. Sometimes conditions change for the group, as with the recreation group, or for a community group that has planned to look at economic development and then a local employer goes out of business. Sometimes it becomes obvious to you as the facilitator that you misunderstood what was being said, that you failed to hear something that was implicit in what was being said, or that you put your own spin on something they were saying. As the group session gets under way you realize that they are resisting or not getting into the flow of things. The planned flow of the meeting suddenly seems wrong. All you can do is to throw it away and go with the emerging current of discussion.

You should not be as flexible when the client cuts drastically into the available time! If you have made plans for a four-hour time slot to surface gaps or problems in an organization's work program and to brainstorm possible new activities and programs to be considered by the planning committee, you cannot flexibly adjust to doing the same work in only two hours. What you can do is to say that if the time frame for group work is now only two hours instead of four, everyone will have to accept that less will be done in facilitated small group session. For example, in the two-hour time frame it might be possible only to identify weaknesses in the current work program and indicate which are the greatest needs—that in the two hours the brainstorming of new actions cannot be accomplished.

SUMMARY

As you design the work session for the group you must remain flexible in order to make adjustments to meet the group's needs. Do not over-design what you will do with the group so that you are over-invested in a particular process and you cannot let go of it. Part of this is technological. Do not get so tied up with a "high tech" method that you cannot adjust if it turns out that a key piece of equipment fails. Additionally, do not assume that using high tech equipment will make up for other deficiencies in your decision making about the design for a meeting. It is true that using computers and projecting a computer image to a public screen with an overhead projector and projection pad system can wow an audience, especially one that has not seen such a system used before or that is not very accustomed to computers. But computers and other slick technology marvels will not make up for imprecise instructions given to small groups nor will they necessarily help to better manage a wandering and out-of-control discussion.

Finally, remember that you will be the party that has the best sense of what is and what is not possible within the time and resources available. You can adjust plans and designs to meet clients' emerging needs but you must also speak forcefully when you believe that requests for changes will compromise the group, its work, or professional standards.

CHAPTER 3

Design for Meeting Space and Equipment

Besides thinking about the process to be used and who will facilitate the break-out groups and all of those other things, the group facilitator and design team must attend to the physical space and equipment for the meeting. It is important to have a room arrangement that will work with the meeting design or at least one that will not unduly compromise what you want to do. The equipment that is brought should cover all contingencies, including possible back-up systems should a critical piece of equipment fail.

MEETING PLACE AND ARRANGEMENTS FOR THE WORK SESSION

An important reason to visit the community ahead of time is to collect information about the issues, expectations, and values that you can use to design an optimal meeting. Similarly, there is tremendous value to visiting the site of the work session prior to the actual group meeting so that you can plan your facilitation to make the most of the physical space or, at least, not be compromised by the limits imposed by the physical space. Obviously, if you have used a facility before, are familiar and comfortable with the rooms that you will occupy, and you know the facility's staff you need not visit the site. A phone conversation may be enough to ensure that the rooms will be properly set up and so on.

When you have never used a particular facility before and

the staff appears unfamiliar with the needs of a facilitated session, it is usually well worth the effort to visit, scope out the
amenities, and talk with the conference coordinator or sales staff.
This will allow you to see the actual size of the rooms, their
layout, availability of break-out space, where breaks and meals
might be, if the participants will have far to walk between break-
out rooms and the main meeting room, whether there is sufficient
electric power for all the equipment you might like to use, and
so on.

Another important thing to do is to sit in the chairs that
the participants will use. As the facilitator you will be spending
most of your time standing. Your colleagues, who may be typing
a running record on a computer or taking notes by hand, and
the participants will spend most of their time sitting. The comfort
or discomfort of the chairs can prove to be a limiting factor in
what you do. Chairs that are covered with a material that does
not breath and that seem to have been designed for use as torture
instruments for the Spanish Inquisition mean that the group will
get tired of the meeting quickly, will have a harder time staying
focused, and will get grumpy. Ergonomically designed chairs will
allow people to sit and work for extended periods of time. Only
by visiting a facility can some of these things be discovered.

By walking around the site and talking to the staff you can
also get a feel for the place. Some facilities have a warm and open
sense that communicates well to a group and invites new thinking. Others are not friendly and the feeling that you get from the
staff is that you will do things their way whether you like it or
not. If you do your checking early on, you can communicate to
the client the suitability and unsuitability of some sites. Later in
the design process, when a decision has been made to use a facility, you can look at what is available or possible and design
the meeting around it and work out a design that makes the most
of the space.

On the following pages there appear some room arrangements that we have found to be good and bad (see Figures 3.1,
3.2, and 3.3). First, *avoid* the arrangements in versions four and
five and other variations on these themes if at all possible (see
Figure 3.3). A facilitated group session is by definition designed

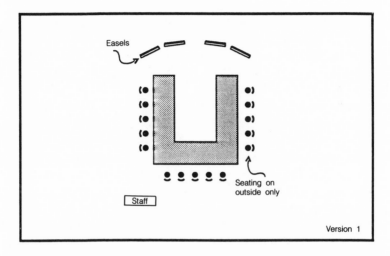

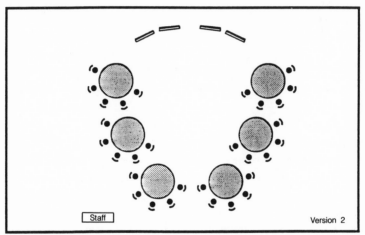

Figure 3.1 *Room arrangements for facilitated group sessions*

to optimize group interaction and discussion in order to work through a particular process. Seats arranged down long, narrow board room tables promote an us versus them orientation that is very good for promoting a management versus labor confrontation. If you must work a group that is seated around a solid table, it is better that the table be round or more square (rather than long and rectangular). Version five is a room that has been

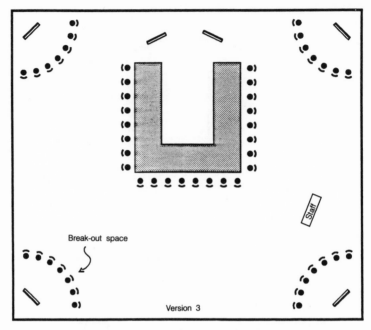

Figure 3.2 *Another room arrangement for facilitated group session*

arranged as a traditional classroom. It is arranged so that people can conveniently see the backs of other peoples' heads. This may promote shooting spit-balls and other junior high school level group activities but it does not promote good group discussion and interaction. Unfortunately, when you talk to facility staff about rooms and they give room capacity figures, these are often for classroom style. You may need to be pushy and almost demand to determine if a room will really hold the size group and seating arrangement that you want.

Versions one, two, and three can be made to work with groups of a variety of sizes. Versions one and three can work with up to 25 or 30 but at that point the horseshoe shape for tables gets very large and above 30 it becomes almost unmanageable. If you plan to work the group as a single group without going to smaller break-out groups and you hope to do that around a single table arrangement, our advice is to keep the

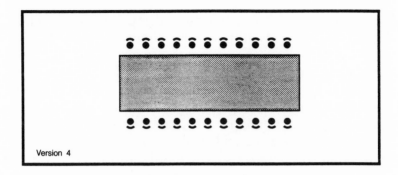

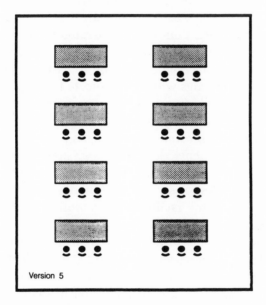

Figure 3.3 *Room arrangements to avoid*

group no larger than 15. Note that version one really requires the use of separate break-out rooms for small group work. Version three uses the corners of a very large room for small group break-out space. While the version three design looks as if it promotes chaos and too much noise, facing the groups into the corners helps to minimize the disruptiveness of the noise and being in the same room tends to promote a certain motivation and competitiveness among the groups. No group wants to look bad and by being able to see that the other groups are generating a lot of ideas, it tends to spur on the groups.

Version two can be used with groups beyond 30. If the tables can be placed so that the round tables are in a rough semicircle, the participants can still engage in some limited large group discussion. The design lends itself to small group tasks and reporting from small groups at each of the tables. Note that no one has been seated at a table with his or her back to the front of the room. This allows everyone to still easily look to the front of the room and focus on the group activity.

When you attempt to communicate your needs to the facility staff or to clients that insist on arranging the room themselves, the best thing to do is to draw a picture. Sketch out what you want. The fax machine allows you to easily transmit these drawings. Your drawings will communicate far better to the actual workers who will set up the meeting rooms. (See Wilson & Hanna, 1990, and especially their Chapter 12, "Groups in Public Settings," for more on room arrangements).

Room arrangements depicted in versions one, two, and three also show a few of the other things that we routinely do. First, we prefer horseshoe style or a group of round tables or any open design so that the facilitators can walk into the midst of the group. For example, if two people at a horseshoe arrangement begin to argue or pontificate across the tables, you can walk into the center of the horseshoe and physically get between them to break that dynamic. The ability to *walk out* into the group allows you as the facilitator to make much greater and more powerful use of your physical presence; walking up close to the group members allows you to focus their attention and break things up. The second point is that each design shows a table for staff. At this table we place the computers(s) and printer and a staff person or two to act as recorders. The table needs to be placed close to electric outlets and yet close enough to the white boards or flip charts so that they can easily read, hear the discussion, and observe the group. Finally, the room must be big enough so that people can get up and walk out of the room while the rest of the group remains at the table working. It also should be big enough for extra chairs to be placed against the walls to provide seating for observers, extra facilitation team staff members, experts who might be called upon to answer a question for the group, and for media representatives. (Because public dollars are frequently used to pay for all or part of these meetings, they will be open to the press and you and the group may have to get used to speaking in front of the media. This is how we often have to operate, much to the amazement of colleagues from Great Britain who do not have to cope with open meeting laws.)

Three final things regarding the space. As one of the last steps in the design or before phase, get to the meeting site early. Rarely is the room set up exactly as you requested. If you get there early enough you can specify your changes to the staff or you can make the changes yourself. By getting there early you will also have time to react to unexpected changes that the facility has imposed on you, such as having moved you to a different and much smaller room without any notice. Second, you should not confuse pseudo-fixed space with fixed space (Steele, 1973). Fixed space, for example, is a room in which the tables and seating are permanently fixed to the floor and cannot be moved. Pseudo-fixed space is a room in which we can actually move things around to accommodate our requirements but we treat it as if it were fixed. Do not put yourself in a bind. Push things around and try some different arrangements. Third, recognize that good work can be done even in bad space. The room arrangement and the chairs will not make or break a work session. The space can make things easier or tougher but you can strive to overcome physical room limitations. We once conducted a very good day-long session with approximately 20 people in a college lecture center/amphitheater where the seats were bolted down and arranged in rising tiers. We had people sit in only the first few rows and spaced within those rows to allow for some give and take discussion. So, be attentive to the physical arrangements but do not only attend to these.

EQUIPMENT

Part of the design is determining what equipment you will need for the group session. The equipment lists that any facilitator develops would be very similar. Certain key items will appear on everyone's list while other items vary due to the technology that a particular facilitator uses. Included is an equipment list (Example 3.1) that was originally developed for a 25-member group that was to break out into three or four small groups.

You can see from the equipment list that we own our own portable easel/flip charts/white boards. These have collapsible legs to fold the device down to roughly the size of a large pad of newsprint. The working surface of the easel is covered with a white board surface to enable a facilitator to work without flip charts and with erasable white board surfaces if he or she prefers. Generally, we have found that it is easier to have our own easels and take them with us than to rely on the facility to provide them. It is clearly cheaper for the client for us to use our own. We are assured of a quality device rather than finding we must use rickety and flimsy units. We also like to take many easels, enough for two for each small group, or four to six easels if we work one larger group. This approach is possible only because we work almost exclusively in-state and travel by car or van and can carry a lot of equipment. Obviously, you can make do with fewer easels, it just means that you will be ripping sheets off and posting them to the wall more frequently. It also means that you might not have enough to give one or two to each small group if you go into break-out sessions.

You can watch office supply catalogues for new product announcements that can make your life easier. For example, *tablets* of plastic sheets that are like pads of newsprint are now available. These plastic sheets can be held to most walls by static electric charges and can be written on with erasable white board markers. These are much more portable than a collection of easels.

Of course, we take pads of newsprint, markers, and tape or other material for sticking sheets up on the walls. Sometimes we use the white board surfaces of the easels and do without pads of newsprint. We may also take computers and associated equipment to allow us to project the computer image to a public screen.

At this point in time we have also gone to using individual small equipment boxes. These are plastic tool boxes or fishing

Example 3.1 *Sample equipment list*

Item	Number Needed
White board easels	8
Permanent marking pens:	
black	12
red	12
green	12
blue	12
Easel pads (3′ by approx. 2′)	12 (includes a few extra)
Masking tape	4 rolls
Scotch tape	1 roll
Duct tape	1 roll (to hold down electric power cables)
Computers	1 or more
Printer	1 (laser printer is preferred due to quality and quiet)
Surge protector	2
Overhead projector	1
Computer projection pad	1
Extension cord	1
Pencils	3 dozen
Paper	3 dozen small pads or a stack of blank scratch paper
Name tents	25 (either preprinted for each participant or blank to be completed by participants)
3″ × 5″ index cards	2 pkg. white, 2 pkg. blue
Scissors	1
Stapler	1
Paper clips	1 box
8 1/2″ × 11″ paper	3 reams (1 ream of 3 different colors)

tackle boxes in which we can carry a variety of marker pens, a roll of masking tape, boxes of pencils, small sheets of paper or 3" by 5" cards, packets of sticking dots (the circular, self-adhesive, and brightly colored dots used for marking file folders), and miscellaneous things like scissors, paper clips, and rubber bands. With personal boxes we each maintain our own supplies and ensure that we do not run out. It is also very convenient just to throw one box of the small stuff in the vehicle and go.

SUMMARY

If you are fortunate enough to have a conference facility for your group session, you will probably find an experienced staff who have already seen most arrangements at one time or another. You can rely quite heavily on these people. If you must use a hotel's ballroom or other facility, you will want to attend more carefully to physical designs and arrangements of the space. Our own experience is that hardly ever can you just walk into the meeting space without having to make some final adjustments. So, arrive early. To be on the safe side, plan to bring much of your own equipment as well.

Part II

The During Phase or What You Do at the Facilitated Session

In this part of the book we present ideas about what goes on during the facilitated meeting. A large number of the groups we have worked with in the past six years were recently organized or they were meeting for the first time. They had no history of meetings. Members did not interact on a regular basis and most participants did not know each other. Fisher and Ellis (1990, p. 19) describe these collections of people as zero-history groups. As a result of working with these groups we pay particular attention to facilitator roles, managing the process, consensus building and problem solving, clarifying expectations and issues, and meeting closure.

For example, regarding facilitator roles, in Chapter 4 we want all attendes of the meeting to feel that it is their agenda and they have had multiple opportunities to participate in all aspects of the meeting. Also of concern is how the facilitator involves experts, manages dominators and conflict, uses small and large group activities to stay on task, and manages meeting time.

In Chapter 5, the facilitator manages the process, that is, he or she starts the meeting, gets the group members to specify *their* procedures (for example, rules) for operation and how people will interact in the facilitated session. Chapter 6 looks at building consensus and group problem solving. A process flow for problem solving is proposed as a general orientation for working with groups.

Helping groups identify and explore their expectations and issues, in Chapter 7, helps to get the groups focused on their agenda. What do *they* want to do at the meeting? Our goal, as discussed in Chapter 8, is to close the meeting with each person knowing exactly what is to be done and who is responsible for getting those jobs done.

CHAPTER 4

Facilitator as Manager of the Process

Facilitators are the managers of the meeting process to accomplish group goals. They are responsible for:

- getting the groups started toward identifying their goals (such as surfacing expectations and building agendas);
- discussing important issues, deciding between which issues should be worked on first and next;
- managing individuals and small groups to surface their best ideas and suggestions;
- guiding the group's activities to minimize the negative dynamics that often reduce a group's potential; and,
- bringing the session to a conclusion with plans for next steps and identifying who will be responsible for which activities between now and the time they meet again.

Facilitators are not responsible for specific decisions made or not made by the group. They can structure a process for bringing issues to the table and the group. They can design small group activities and tasks to get people involved in discussion of these problems. They are not responsible for decisions made by the group regarding individual issues.

MANAGING VIA JUDICIOUS INTERVENTIONS

The discussion that follows explores ways for the facilitator to manage the group session flow with different techniques. It should be understood that the group process is like a flow and that what the facilitator does is to observe that flow and then decide whether to intervene to affect the direction and force of that flow. When things seem to be going well, the facilitator's proper function is to stay out of the way of that flow. The correct function at those times is to help the group by taking notes on the flip charts and to simply not impede the flow. Sometimes the facilitator observes and senses that the group flow is not what it could be. At those times the facilitator then plays a more active role by intervening into the group functioning and seeking to redirect the flow or to affect its speed, either slowing it down or hurrying it along. The interventions should be directed to the particular needs of the specific group at a certain point in time. An intervention may address conflict that is emerging in the group, the group's attempt to skip an important step in the process, the need to break through barriers limiting creativity, and so on.

A general rule of thumb is that the facilitator should be willing to use lower level interventions and to minimize the number of interventions (Corey, Corey, Callahan, & Russell, 1988). At times the facilitator must remind himself or herself to remain quiet and to allow the group members to pour their energies into the group deliberations and to control the flow themselves. The following information on managing the process should be considered in light of this view of the facilitator as intervenor.

MANAGING THE PROCESS

Facilitators are often described as the meeting chauffeur, the meeting manager, the process manager and by other terms which imply a management function. As a meeting manager the facilitator is *neutral* to the agenda, that is, she or he does not have a vested interest in the content of the group's agenda. However, we believe the facilitators are aggressive toward the process, that is, they manage: meeting time, process techniques, meeting flow, timing of breaks and meals, and the group's work toward satisfying their needs.

Group management can involve several issues, such as:

- getting started, icebreakers, and social events;
- evaluating and critiquing ideas;
- monitoring meeting information;
- managing side conversations within the meeting; and
- accommodating meeting latecomers.

Getting Started

If the facilitated meeting is scheduled to get underway at 8:30 a.m. we do our best to start on time to set a standard. We begin building credibility with the group at each meeting by doing what we said we would do! Assuming most, if not all people, are in the room and seated around the U-shaped arrangement of tables (see Figures 3.1, 3.2, and 3.3) and are ready to go, we like to have *name tents* at each place (and we are prepared to make additional tents if someone comes in unexpectedly). For some groups you may want the group members to make their name tents, be creative in design, color, use of favorite nicknames, and provide a message or favorite quote. This gives the group members a chance to say who they are.

Icebreaker

An icebreaker activity might be appropriate at this time to get people into the spirit of the meeting (Forbess-Greene, 1983). We want them to begin thinking about the project they are working on (say . . . locating a solid waste site/dump in their community). For example, we might use a modified brainwriting exercise (see Example 4.1) where we give each person two sheets of paper (one white and one blue) and ask all of them to list three words that describe their *concerns* (about the dump sites) on the white sheet and three words to describe their *expectations* about the meeting on the blue. Give them time (say 2 or 3 minutes) to write down their individual responses and then ask them to meet with two other people to introduce themselves and discuss what they wrote. In the small groups we might ask them to report only

Example 4.1 *Brainwriting Technique*

Brainwriting (Nutt, 1989) is a technique for the generation of ideas that separates the generation step from the evaluation step. It differs from brainstorming in that individuals are instructed to write their ideas rather that to simply yell them out. The way that we typically use it is to give group members letter size sheets of paper, from as few as one to as many as nine. A question is stated to the group, for example, "What specific actions might be taken by parties in our community to keep students in school rather than dropping out?" Group members are asked to write one idea per sheet of paper. Group members are told to write with wide tipped marker, to use as few words as possible to get the idea down, and to use large lettering so that it is easy to see. Often before they begin to write, we hold up an example of a properly written sheet with a few words written in large letters and an example that has been done poorly. After individuals have finished, a round robin technique can be used to get one idea at a time from each individual and to post it on the wall with tape or other material. Identical or very similar ideas can be clustered together to one spot on the wall while different ideas can be separated from one another. The group can easily observe the development of their ideas on the wall and can suggest where an item might best be posted. When all items have been posted on the wall the group can review the result, suggest how some sheets might be moved to create a better sorting of ideas, indicate that something is missing and needs to be added, or be voted upon to determine which items are the best, of highest priority, or need to be addressed first.

This brainwriting technique can serve a facilitator well. For one thing it frees the facilitators from having to write down all of their ideas onto flip charts. Further, it allows for a very easy sorting of ideas or clustering of ideas into categories. Rather than scratching out a couple lines of writing on a flip chart and rewriting the idea next to a related item, a sheet can simply be moved. The technique also allows for variations. If the facilitator senses that there may be a need to generate ideas anonymously the sheets with ideas can be collected, placed into a common pile, shuffled, and then either posted to the wall from the pile or passed back out to individuals for a round robin posting. If the facilitator is concerned that some group members may be illiterate or not very facile at writing, small groups can be used to generate ideas and write them on sheets. The ideas can then be processed from the small groups to the wall. Different color sheets of paper can be used for different tasks or to designate other differences. For example, participants might be given three colors of paper and be asked to write assets on one color, liabilities on another color, and necessary actions on a third color.

three concerns, so there must be some discussion and some agreement, possibly consensus, about which three concerns are reported by their group.

The next activity would be to use a modification of the nominal group technique (NGT) (see Example 4.2) to ask for one concern from each group in a round robin fashion until all items on the groups' lists are recorded. Participants would be asked to discuss these concerns and facilitators may want to indicate how they will be addressed by the meeting's activities and processes. This list of concerns should remain visible to the group as a reminder throughout the meeting.

Other icebreakers we find helpful in creating energy within the group include having participants write newspaper headlines describing the outcomes or results of the meeting. Also we have asked group members to pair up, interview and introduce one another to the group by sharing information about their place of residence in the community, elected or appointed positions, occupation, and something interesting, such as hobbies or special interests or community concerns. Sometimes we ask participants to use one or two words to describe their reasons for attending the meeting. These one or two words often identify concerns or, possibly, hidden agendas of members which can be addressed by the group. Another exercise we might use is to have individuals or teams draw a picture about what they think the "new" community ought to look like or what the organization would look like when the project is completed.

We generally prefer to use icebreaker exercises that are related to the groups' tasks, rather than exercises that are more touchy-feely for the group or more disconnected from the task of the group. This is an admitted bias on our part and not all facilitators feel the same way that we do. A wide range of exercise designs are available (for example, University Associates Handbooks for Facilitators, 1972–1991; VanGundy, 1988; Nutt,

Example 4.2   *Nominal Group Technique (NGT)*

Delbecq, Van de Ven, and Gustafson (1975) present this technique for involving all group members in the process. The technique limits and constrains group interaction in order to limit the opportunities for individual domination or other process losses. The technique involves a sequence of simple steps. They are:

1. silent generation of ideas by individuals in response to a facilitator read question;
2. recording of ideas on flip charts as individuals take turns reporting one of their ideas in a round robin procedure that continues until all members pass or have no other ideas to report;
3. a review of the list to ensure that all members understand the ideas but that does not allow a debate of the worthiness of the ideas;
4. a secret balloting to allow individuals to indicate what they think are the best ideas on the list;
5. a review of the results of the balloting with discussion; and
6. a second round of balloting, if it is necessary.

This technique was developed to use in groups in which there were significant differences in verbal competency, status differentials, and other characteristics that would limit some participants' ability to participate and allow others to unduly dominate. The steps to the process were developed to allow all to participate but severely limit the ability of individuals to dominate the group.

This technique has had wide application and continues to be used extensively today. An infinite number of variations appears to be possible on the basic scheme of the technique. For example, pairs or small groups of individuals can be used to accomplish the initial generation of ideas. Or individuals can generate their ideas and then be placed into small groups to perform an initial sort of their ideas and remove any redundant items. Or during the reporting of the ideas step the facilitator can continually ask for ideas that are different from the ideas already captured on the list in order to limit the recording of duplicates. Or variations on voting can be used, for example, public voting by making check marks next to the good ideas can be used or time can be allowed for discussion and lobbying prior to the voting. The basic robustness of the technique allows for variations to meet specific group needs or to simply change the process so that it does not become stale.

1989) and can be customized for the particular group. The purpose of using a variety of icebreakers and group exercises is to take time for members to get to know each other. By sharing information and working cooperatively on problem-solving exercises or games the group members learn to trust each other and create a climate for collaboration.

Social Event or Reception

The purpose of a reception (for example, the night before or at 11:00 a.m. before the official kickoff luncheon or at a continental breakfast or some other get acquainted activity) is to have the participants meet each other and the facilitators and to feel comfortable about the up-coming meeting. This is especially useful when working with zero-history groups (Fisher & Ellis, 1990). A potential spinoff benefit would be for participants to begin building informal communication networks.

As often as possible we like to specify, on the invitation letter (to the facilitated meeting) and on printed agendas, that the room will be open for participants to have coffee or soft drinks 30 minutes before the actual meeting begins. This time can be used for informal meetings, networking, and so on. We begin *promptly* as indicated on the invitation letter and/or printed agenda. See Figure 4.1 for an example of the type of printed agenda we prefer to use. Our intent is to get people to the session on time. By specifying we will begin promptly at an announced time (for example, coffee at 8:30 a.m. first session at 9:00 a.m.) those who arrive on time are not penalized by having to wait on people who might be late.

Ensuring That All Have the Chance to Participate

The key difference between a regular meeting and a facilitated meeting is the assurance that everyone is encouraged and that procedures are used to offer many opportunities for *all* group members to participate and express their views about

COMMUNITY DEVELOPMENT MEETING
September 23–24

SCHEDULE

Monday, September 23

8:30 A.M.	Coffee and rolls
9:00 A.M.	Work Session with break
12:00 Noon	Lunch
1:00 P.M.	Work Session with break
5:00 P.M.	Adjourn

Tuesday, September 24

8:30 A.M.	Coffee and rolls
9:00 A.M.	Work Session with break
12:00 Noon	Lunch
1:00 P.M.	Work Session with break
5:00 P.M.	Adjourn

Figure 4.1 *Preprinted Schedule*

ideas, issues, problems, solutions, decisions, and plans of action.
If all group members do not participate, why bother to conduct
a facilitated meeting? Our view of participation in a community
meeting is that it is important to tap into the knowledge and
perceptions of the people selected to attend. They should be given
every opportunity to contribute to the discussion and decision
making in the meeting.

It is essential that all members of the group feel that they
can make a contribution to the discussion and to the decision-
making process. Facilitators use a variety of techniques to demonstrate that all members are expected to contribute to
discussions and meeting outcomes. For example, the nominal
group technique (NGT), see Example 4.2, is often used to get
people involved in the meeting. There are many variations of this

procedure but it usually includes having each member pause and individually respond to a question or problem situation and write down on paper responses to, for example, "list three uses of the report from this meeting." Participants may be asked to share one item from their list, by going around the meeting table from member to member, until all items on all lists are recorded on newsprint. After reviewing the list, the facilitator may ask for one additional item from each member as a way of trying to exhaust the possible uses for the report. This technique, designed by Delbecq, Van de Ven, and Gustafson (1975), was to make sure that all group members were given equal opportunity to identify items and to add these items for group discussion without being criticized by the group.

Facilitators may use other approaches such as asking for contributions from those group members who have remained silent for a period of time. This is not to be confused with calling on one particular group member, putting that person on the spot, and forcing him or her to contribute or to look foolish. As the facilitator you must not attempt to force people to participate or to embarrass an individual.

Using small groups is another way of offering more possibilities for "air time." In small groups more individuals can talk at the same time about an issue or problem. If group members seem uncomfortable with their supervisors or bosses in the same meeting, it may be necessary to define small groups, "as the group without your boss or supervisor," so it's ok and expected for you to move to the group that doesn't include your boss.

Establish the norm that group members are expected to participate in all of the meeting activities but they can *pass* if they want to. However, if an individual passes on everything then the facilitator and/or group leader may want to discuss the situation with that person or with the group. Is it acceptable to the group that this one person does not contribute? Would this one person rather not be there at all? Would the group prefer to allow the person to just sit in and observe? The point is that it might be better to address the continual passing of one person in an open and direct manner.

Experts to Inform the Group

Often groups will address an issue that they think requires expert information before they feel fully informed to make a decision or recommendation. The challenge for facilitators in this situation is to have the group fully explore the issue, designate which parts of the issue require expert information, and bring the expert into the conversation without allowing him or her to dominate the discussion. An approach to involving experts is to have them attend the meeting but not sit at the table with group members. The experts' role is to listen to the conversation, reflect upon the issue, and respond to questions posed by the group (either managed by the facilitator or a member of the group). The facilitator can assist in the questioning process by encouraging the group members to be specific about their information needs and to write down (on newsprint/flip charts) questions for the expert. This directs the expert to a specific list of topics for comment and discussion. The expert should respond to only those questions which the group has presented and the information can be readily applied to decision making. Ideally you as facilitator or the group's leadership will identify experts who can be both sensitive to the group process and have the information needed by the group in its deliberations.

Dominating Individuals

Groups can sometimes find themselves being dominated, intimidated, and monopolized by a single individual or small group. Managing these situations can be a challenge to the novice or skilled facilitator. There are many options for controlling the *dominating* individual or small group. One approach might be to acknowledge what the individual is saying, record it on newsprint, and go to the next person for comments. Another approach might be to sum up the dominator's point of view and ask for another person's comments. The facilitator might say, "We need to hear from all people at the table before getting a second point from any member of the group." The facilitator may suggest that small groups discuss several issues including the dominator's concern. We hope that later the group members will respond to the dominator, if he or she persists, explaining that small groups have discussed the topic, reached consensus on it, and decided to move on.

Some more *drastic measures* for managing dominating individuals include (after the dominator has continued to take up too much time for his or her issue):

- deliberately pacing the discussion and turning to other group members by asking for comments, thereby involving the whole group in enforcing rules regarding participation;
- using a strict adherence to the nominal group technique (NGT), see Example 4.2, to get more people involved in the discussion;
- not writing down on newsprint what the dominator is saying or pointing out where these issues have already been recorded;
- stopping the session and clarifying again what the task is and how the task is to be completed;
- calling for a group break to change the dynamics of the session;
- using a recall/repeat technique, such as requiring that before a group member can make a point he or she must summarize the two previous comments about this issue;
- at the break, speaking to the dominators and checking for their understanding of the need for everyone to be able to participate; and
- asking the group leader to request that the dominator leave the meeting, as a last resort, if the dominator threatens to disrupt the meeting.

As a facilitator you must admit to yourself that you are *not* all powerful and cannot bring everyone into line. Unfortunately, some of our worst experiences have been with some state senators and state representatives acting as members of community groups. Our painful experience is that too often these individuals feel compelled to comment at length, demonstrate their knowledge, and inform their constituents about every issue mentioned. Some of these elected officials choose not to pick up on subtle signs from the group or facilitator that they are being less than helpful. A few of them have been impervious to even very blunt requests as well. All you can do is try.

Reading the Group

At times facilitators may appear to ask stupid or obvious questions and check in with group members to ask for guidance and clarification. Knowing when to ask those obvious questions is sometimes referred to as *reading the group*. The facilitator may have overheard a side conversation, seen a puzzled look on a participant's face, heard a small group discuss the need for moving on to the next part of the meeting, or sense concern that the group is bogging down. Facilitators are continually looking, listening, and trying to get a feeling about how the meeting is progressing. Does it look, sound, and feel as if the group members are working on the tasks that will get them to their desired outcome or end result?

Reading the group may be accomplished by asking simple questions. Are we working on the topics, issues, and tasks that will get us to our goal by 8:00 p.m.? We accomplished a lot of our agenda this morning, so for the afternoon session do we continue on with item #6 or do we need to select other items which are more important for accomplishing our meeting goal by 8:00 p.m.? We believe it is important to study the group members, their reactions, body language, discussion, attention to meeting tasks, and the overall process. But it is equally important to verbally check in with the group and get agreement and permission to change activities. Do not use some mysterious process of viewing nonverbal behaviors and then announcing what will be done. Your reading of the nonverbal cues might be on target or might suggest the wrong message.

Managing Conflict in the Group

A facilitator must be able to look upon the positive and the negative aspects of conflict. He or she must be able to consider the need to reduce, limit, and channel conflict or to enhance, make explicit, and amplify the conflict. We address management of conflict in this sense of duality, rather than simply assuming that conflict is always bad and should be eliminated. Generally, we attempt to keep conflict from becoming a series of personal attacks. We clearly indicate that attacking individuals for who they are is not a condoned behavior. However, we allow and encourage conflict about ideas.

The approach that we take to problem solving inherently accepts a problem-solving approach to dealing with conflict. Thomas and Kilmann (1974), among a variety of authors who have addressed conflict, report that people react in five basic ways regarding interpersonal conflict:

- competing—satisfy your concerns at the expense of others (for example, win-lose situations);
- collaborating—satisfy both parties concerns (for example, win-win situations);
- compromising—each side gives up something to gain something (for example, lose-win situations);
- avoiding—indifferent to their own concerns and others concerns (for example, lose-lose situations); and
- accommodating—more concerned with pleasing others than with meeting their needs (for example, ambiguous situations).

For us facilitation of groups normally entails the attempt to create a collaborative approach to dealing with conflict. For example, if the conflict that emerges is between two solutions and there seems to be division over which of the two is better, we will engage the group in a process that seeks to creatively find additional solutions or to merge the alternatives into a hybrid that combines the best of the two original alternatives. (See Chapter 6 for a section of group problem solving.) The intent is to use the conflict of ideas to spur the group to better and richer idea generation and perhaps to even break the group out of an old paradigm. Additionally, moving the group from a consideration of two particular and competing solutions and to a discussion at a policy level of what would a good solution look like may help the group to make productive use of its conflict.

It is naive and erroneous to assume that more or deeper communication will automatically resolve conflict. It is possible that better communication will eliminate conflict that is due to differences in perceptions or misunderstandings of what other people want. However, more communication may allow two parties to come to a better understanding that they have completely different sets of values and that they desire different things from a solution. Communication in this case will help to clarify the conflict, not make it go away; this may be helpful to the overall meeting process.

As the facilitator you can attempt to get the group to collaborate, to explore for win-win solutions, and to create more alternatives. You can help to clarify what is wanted to see if the conflict is due to real differences or due to errors in perception. At times as a facilitator you may have to help the group to agree to disagree. There may be something about which the group cannot agree. You can suggest that such an issue be tabled for the moment and be reconsidered later in the meeting. Having worked through other issues and concerns may have cleared space for the group to now resolve the conflict. It is also possible that the group now better understands that the issue is not resolvable and needs to be left alone.

Monitoring Meeting Time

Facilitators monitor both the agenda and time available for the meeting. Facilitators can become too attached by trying to rigidly and compulsively work through the full agenda in the time available. However, these are two of the concerns that are important to conducting a successful meeting. One of the first activities for a facilitated meeting is establishing the working agenda out of participant expectations or issues. From this exercise it is possible to get an idea of work activities for the meeting or session. We believe it is important to establish a climate for discussion, sharing, and consensus building within the group. Part of this climate building is to demonstrate, throughout the meeting, that the group is in charge or responsible for items on the agenda and the facilitator is responsible for reminding the group of its progress and time available to discuss and decide issues. One approach for time management is to keep the group informed of decisions made and how much time there is available to complete remaining tasks. Periodically, facilitators may want to stop and ask the group or obtain agreement from the group on which items to discuss in the remaining time frame for the meeting. Identifying and periodically clarifying the priority items still on the list or agenda will help to ensure that the time available is allocated to the most important issues.

Breaks and Small Group Assignments

Sometimes the energy level of the group is low so we take a break, get something to eat, change the group dynamics, or use an icebreaker exercise to renew interest in a topic and move on toward achieving some part of the group's agenda or goals.

When we use small groups we very clearly and precisely define what the group is to do and the process to be used in reporting to the large group. Most of the time we write the group assignment on white boards/flip charts so all can refer to what is to be done. One of the purposes for not using a rigid and timed agenda or schedule is to allow facilitators flexibility in calling breaks, small group work, and the like when they are needed, rather than using a preset schedule.

It may sound funny to say but calling a break is almost never a bad thing to do. It changes the dynamics. It gives you a chance to quietly consider what was going on and possibly what was going wrong. A break is a great opportunity to confer with a team member and figure out next steps or a change of roles.

HELPING THE GROUP MAINTAIN FOCUS

Checking in

Checking in is a technique used during small group sessions, as well as within the large group, to see if the information and the process is meeting eveyone's needs. In this technique the facilitator may ask the following:

- Have you (the group/individual members) had the opportunity to express your concern about the topic?
- Have the small groups identified all the parts of this issue so you (individual members and the group) can make a decision?
- Has the large group discussion identified more topics that need clarification or discussion about the issue?
  - If yes, list these topics and ask the group if they want to discuss them farther;
  - If no, then move on to the next topic for discussion.

The checking-in process with the group includes RCA (*r*estating the issue, concern, or question, *c*larifying the issue by the group and seeking *a*greement that the issue needs more discussion or moving on to the next topic on the agenda).

Staying on Task

One of the issues often raised by facilitators and clients is: how do we keep the group on task? Related concerns include: how do you recognize the need to stop or redirect the discussion and "how do you keep from chasing rabbits" (that is, topics not relevant to the task)? Other questions along this line of thought include:

- What are the indicators that a group is wandering from its task?
- How do you redirect the group without being argumentative?

- What if members of the group want to discuss too many issues at the same time?
- What do you do if the group thinks the meeting agenda is unrealistic? (However, the facilitator usually feels this, *not* the group.)

Staying on task, (see Example 4.3) begins with initial discussions about the need for a facilitated meeting and becomes the basis for managing the group process. Discussing the reasons for having the group meet and possible outcomes of the session help to shape the *tasks*. Establishing ground rules with group members is the beginning of identifying and isolating factors which may distract the group from achieving its tasks, for example, criticizing ideas rather than brainstorming or holding side conversations when others in the group are talking. Asking the group to talk about expectations for today's meeting is a technique to begin building the group's agenda, not the sponsor's or the facilitator's perception of what ought to be discussed. Working with the group to categorize and then to prioritize (for example, by using ratings, such as, what is economically feasible and what is politically feasible) issues for the agenda is another way of getting the group to establish *ownership* and responsibility for working on their ideas. As the group begins to focus on one or two issues to begin their discussion it may be appropriate to use small group assignments to get more people talking at the same time on a specific issue.

Staying on task is really utilizing the group process to specify what the group wants to talk about and using techniques to identify its issues so the agenda is *owned* by the group and staying on task becomes part of its responsibility. As previously mentioned, the facilitator *checks in* with the group to confirm that activities are reaching objectives. Another way to visually reinforce this process is to keep group expectations, issues, or the agenda on newsprint/flip chart paper taped on the walls in the meeting room to emphasize individual ideas and the group's desire to work on selected issues. Occasionally revisiting the list and asking if we are progressing as we should or merely spinning our wheels, can be helpful.

Example 4.3   *Helping the group stay on task*

1. Remind the groups of their ground rules.
2. Keep the assignment posted and visible.
3. The facilitator can/should interject into the discussion at times when it seems to be rambling), "How does this seem to relate to our assignment?"
4. Ask participants to clarify their statements and how they relate to the task at hand. Say, "Could you help me understand how that relates to X, for the record?"
5. Monitor the passage of time and reevaluate the priorities and tasks based on the time available.
6. Assign another facilitation team member to monitor staying on task.
7. Write down only the relevant points on flip charts/white boards.
8. Put different (that is, nonrelevant) topics on a separate chart and let the group decide whether to come back to those later. Label the items *other*, *parking lot*, A-*ha's*, or have the group name the label.
9. Provide decision points or milestones in the process.
10. Use the RCA (restate, clarify and seek agreement) technique.

Facilitators are constantly touching base with the group to reconfirm progress and interest in continuing to work on an issue or problem. If the group is in agreement to continue with the discussion about water and sewer problems, then stay on that issue. However, individuals or small groups may want to change directions and shift the discussion to zoning regulations that specify water runoff and sewerage standards. Does the facilitator change directions? Not just yet. Is it the desire of the *entire group* to make the shift from one topic to another? If about two thirds want to shift topics can the other third be accommodated by coming back to the water and sewer issue after some preliminary discussion about zoning regulations? If so, then the *group has decided* to change directions rather than the facilitator becoming the group leader, thereby changing roles to push the group in a direction that it may not want to go.

It is important to keep the agenda and changes to the agenda visible for the group so that members can monitor their own progress and point out the need to revisit issues if that was the previously agreed upon strategy. In some instances, say on the second day of a 2- or 3-day group session, it may be advantageous to rebuild the agenda recognizing what was accomplished the first day and what needs to be accomplished the second and third days to achieve all members' expectations.

Using Preprinted Schedules or Meeting Flow Charts

In some situations groups like to have a preprinted meeting schedule (see Figure 4.1). We like facilitators to have as much flexibility as possible when planning and conducting meetings. People have remarked that our preprinted agendas only include " . . . when to start, when to work, when to eat, when to take a break and when to adjourn." Often we are not as specific about the breaks, preferring to place them within the work sessions. Another example (see Figure 4.2) of a preprinted schedule or meeting plan, we are beginning to use, illustrates the flow and purpose of the meeting without limiting the facilitator's options to call breaks and redirect the group to use different exercises when needed. The county planning session preprinted agenda can be changed (for example, substitute environmental scanning report with an icebreaker) to reflect what the group wants and indicate some of the techniques that facilitators might use to initiate discussion. Small and large group activities are indicated as well as suggesting next steps and closing or adjourning the meeting. What is omitted from this example are specific times (such as, 10:00 a.m. break, 11:30 small group work, and so on) when work activities will be started or changed. We want to give as much information about the meeting while at the same time reserving the facilitator's flexibility to use a variety of approaches to set priorities (for instance, secret balloting or other techniques appropriate to the group and situation).

SUMMARY

If all group members have an opportunity to participate on all aspects of the meeting, has the facilitator's job been accomplished? The answer is yes and no. When involving multiple per-

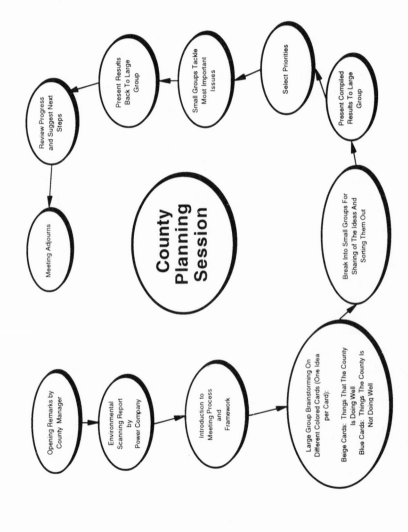

Figure 4.2 *County planning session*

sonalities from various segments of a community or organization there will be differences of opinion on what can and should be done about an issue. Managing these different viewpoints, orientations, and perceptions while not alienating individuals or the group is the facilitator's primary task. The facilitator manages the group by directing its energies toward meeting its agenda.

CHAPTER 5

Setting the Rules for the Game

We believe that setting and using ground rules is the single most important way that facilitators can be proactive and even be preemptive in working with the group to establish acceptable behavior patterns in the facilitated session. Without a set of agreed-upon ground rules, the facilitator will be having to react to inappropriate behaviors and play a constant catch-up game.

GROUND RULES

We use the *Ten Commandments* (see Example 5.1) with groups as a way of efficiently using their important time during the meeting. We do not lay these on a group without first introducing them as having emerged from our work with groups and how they have helped all groups, especially the zero-history groups, establish their operating procedures.

The role of facilitator includes discussing options for achieving intended outcomes or purposes prior to the session. These are further specified and reviewed with participants within the group in the form of *operating procedures* or sometimes called *ground rules*. How does the group want to conduct business during the group work session? We suggest that facilitators should be neutral to the content of the agenda. The agenda is basically the content of what the client or group wants to achieve. The facilitator should not have a solution or hidden agenda that he or she is trying to sell the group. However, we assert that facilitators become aggressive to the process! Facilitators should

Example 5.1   *Ten Commandments*

1. Thou shalt participate fully.
2. Thou shalt actually listen to what others say.
3. Thou shalt accept what others say as valid.
4. Thou shalt share responsibility for making this meeting a success.
5. Even if thou art the expert, thou shalt not dictate.
6. During brain storming, thou shalt not censor thyself or others.
7. Thou shalt encourage fresh ideas, new perspectives, and crazy notions.
8. Thou shalt ensure that thy words are captured on the flip charts.
9. Thou shalt respect the process.
10. Thou shalt realize that this retreat is only the start and that you must be committed to follow through.

apply, direct, and control the process for accomplishing the goals or outcomes of the group.

Rather than wait for the group to decide on the process, we suggest facilitators start with some discussion and specification of group ground rules such as the Ten Commandments. These ten commandments were developed in a humorous vein to provide a set of rules for a group but in a manner that was light and user-friendly.

Enforcing Rules

The keepers of the ground rules are members of the group. Group enforcement is made easier by using balled up sheets of 8 1/2 × 11 paper thrown in the direction of a group member or facilitator or group leader to indicate that this person has violated a ground rule and must adjust his or her behavior to the group's agreed-upon standards of communication and conduct. Group enforcement of the ground rules is a powerful tool for keeping on task and acknowledging that the group is in control. Groups need to be given a chance to play with throwing the balls and get comfortable with the behavior. One of the facilitators can purposely break a rule to allow everyone a practice throw.

Customizing Rules

If we build ground rules from scratch we may start with the following cuing questions: "how do you want to conduct this meeting throughout the next two days?" "Do you want to establish any procedures or ground rules for conducting this meeting?" If you get back blank stares from participants we suggest the following:

• create an atmosphere of trust so that we trust each other not to start gossip or rumors or adverse conversations about what individuals or the groups discuss in their efforts to reach decisions or solve problems at this facilitated meeting;
• unless otherwise directed by the facilitator, all ideas from any participant are ok! . . . (we're not here to criticize personalities or ideas but to look at alternatives for problem solving and decision making);
• list ideas and recommendations from the group . . . check them out to see if ALL participants agree to these as ground rules or rules for meeting operations; and
• if all else fails to get the group started with its own rules or procedures you may want to suggest the Ten Commandments or the 15 rules described below for the group to consider.

When developing ground rules for a group we consider the following checklist (see Example 5.2) to get the group to consider issues, procedures and problems.

It is expected that the group will either develop its own rules (mentioned previously as starting from scratch), adopt existing rules (for example, Ten Commandments), or modify existing rules (for example, the 15) to meet their own needs. If the group adopts a fast, rubber stamp, set of rules without discussion and some modifications, this behavior could be an indication that the group has not accepted ownership of the meeting. Facilitators will want to take time to review, discuss, and modify rules to reflect group ownership of the meeting.

As we have worked with other groups we have added to, deleted from, substituted, and modified items on the ten commandment list, thereby, arriving at the list of 15 rules. The 15

Example 5.2 *Checklist for Customizing Facilitation Ground Rules*

Rules depend on the client, nature of project, or what features of project need to be addressed, such as:

___ Purpose of the meeting
___ Meeting results
___ Group composition
___ Group size—minimum number, maximum number
___ Time blocks for the sessions or facilitated meetings
___ Client and facilitator responsibilities
___ Content of the meeting announcement
___ Physical environment and facility limitations
___ Project, process, and requirement
___ Meeting format, number of facilitators

Group concerns and issues.

___ Desired meeting result (e.g., plan of action)
___ Participant expectations
___ Time frames for the retreat/meeting
___ Opinions are welcomed and valued
___ Work together in cooperative venture
___ Facilitator's role
___ Absences, tardiness of participants
___ Consequences for violating rules
___ Rights and responsibilities of participants

Nature of meeting/project

___ Educational
___ Open forum
___ Expert presentation
___ Closed forum
___ Other

rules seems to be more comprehensive but the humorous presentation has been lost. Our experience is that the facilitator needs to be careful about how the 15 rules are presented. It is easy for the discussion to get to heavy so that the rules are no longer perceived as aids for improving the meeting but as mean-spirited barriers.

Example 5.3 *Fifteen Customized Rules*

These rules will help ensure that this is a productive meeting.

1. Actively listen to each other.
2. Respect what others say and their points of view—recognize that no one has a monopoly on the truth.
3. Personal attacks of any kind are not allowed.
4. Actively participate.
5. Focus on the doable.
6. Be specific and ensure meaningfulness.
7. Look for common ground.
8. Focus on what can be done to remedy things—after the problem definition step, stop the complaining and blaming and get to what you can do.
9. No side conversations—share your thoughts.
10. Maintain an outcome orientation.
11. Stay resourceful—think creatively.
12. If you get stuck, move on—don't allow yourselves to get bogged down.
13. Accept that this meeting is just the start.
14. Enforcing rules is everyone's responsibility.
15. No booze until the work is done.

KEY RULES THAT MIGHT NEED EMPHASIS

The following four rules might deserve some special attention, especially depending upon the group. We caution some groups that we work with on these in particular.

When to Evaluate and Critique?

In many sessions the facilitator may say, "Brainstorm ideas first without criticizing the idea so we can get may viewpoints expressed, then we can go·through the list and add to, eliminate, combine, and critique our ideas." The basic problems with getting individuals within a group to share ideas are: their fears that they may be or appear to be wrong; that others will not like their ideas; or that someone may challenge their viewpoint. We suggest that one of the critical ground rules be to suspend evaluation of ideas and critiquing until all of the viewpoints are expressed (Delbecq, Van de Ven, & Gustafson, 1975; Nutt, 1989). Once the group has finished brainstorming (see Example 5.4) all the ideas or alternatives, the group can logically turn to reviewing and evaluating ideas. We suggest that the group be encouraged to look for common ground within the ideas, focus on what is doable, understand what the idea means, and clarify as ideas are reviewed. Then at an appropriate time in the meeting the group may want to go through all items as a whole and use some standard or group specified criteria for evaluating and critiquing ideas.

Meeting Information

"What is said stays here!" We recommend that group members recognize the need for some discussion and information to stay within the group. In other words, the conversations, issues, discussions, critiques, and information shared ought to stay within the group and not to be used by group members for gossip or for "unfair" advantage back home.

If the group adopts this idea of "what is said stays here" as a ground rule then it will need to describe what is acceptable behavior for members both in the meeting and back home in their community (assuming they may be attending a group session in an another location). We raise this concern from the viewpoint of making sure that information disseminated from a particular meeting is accurate and timely. Typically, a group may set as a policy that brainstormed ideas are not intended for distribution and external discussion.

Timeliness is probably more of a problem than accuracy. In some situations a group may want to meet to discuss issues for several weeks before identifying possible solutions and making decisions about possible outcomes. It is difficult to keep people in the community informed about the discussions without creating speculation about solutions and outcomes.

Side Conversations

In our opinion, side conversations between group members during a meeting are a most distracting and rude display of behavior. Recall how your school teachers waited until the two or three people completed their discussion before proceeding. Unfortunately, this may not work with adults. Address the issue with the group, "The purpose of this meeting is for all of us listen to each other and understand different views about community issues, what you share with the person beside you would be of interest to the entire group!" If this is an accepted ground rule then the facilitator and group can enforce it by a variety of methods, such as: speaking directly to the parties or by taking a short break to speak to the individuals about their disruption.

In some instances, however, side conversations are an indicator of group restlessness and the need to move on to other topics. If this behavior persists, stop the side discussions! Ask for clarification from the group about how to deal with this situation. Redirect group activities to meet their goals or expectations or take a break, as appropriate.

Ways to stop side conversations include:

• letting the group enforce its own rules;
• have the facilitator ask for clarification about member behavior;
• arrange small group work activities to get more people talking at the same time;
• have the facilitator stand behind the conversing parties;
• have the facilitator get between the talkers to block their view; and,
• ask the discussants to openly share their ideas and reinforce that we hope to hear from all group members regarding the particular issue.

Meeting Latecomers or Absentees

When someone comes in late we do stress that he or she must be willing to accept the group's expectations, directions,

Example 5.4 *Brainstorming*

Studies indicate that creativity can be stimulated by using simple and practical exercises. Brainstorming is designed to give participants an opportunity to engage in a creative problem-solving exercise. Unfortunately, in many instances the spark of innovative thinking is dampened by killer phrases like "We tried it last year," "We've always done it that way," "They tried it in Albany and it didn't work there," and a host of similar comments.

To acclimate participants by flicking on their innate green light of creativity, a simple brainstorm session should be used. The basic ground rules of brainstorming are:

1. No critical judgment is permitted.
2. Free-wheeling is welcomed (that is, the wilder the idea, the better).
3. Quantity, not quality is desired.
4. Combinations and improvement of ideas are sought (Van-Gundy, 1984, pp. 171–172).

We have asked groups to brainstorm using modifications of the above description. We always specify the basic ground rules and even write these down on white boards/flip chart paper to keep in front of the group. Sometimes we may use energizer exercises (such as connect the nine dots, what does a paper clip look like . . . a race track . . . and so on) to get participants to loosen up and feel that they have permission to be creative and crazy.

Small groups of 5 to 8 people are given a flip chart and directed to list as many ideas as possible in two minutes about a problem or issue (for example, what do we need to do to: (1) improve the downtown business district; (2) change the traffic pattern near the proposed high school; (3) get more people involved in the "clean and beautiful" campaign for the county?). We get the small groups to share their list of ideas with each other, discuss them briefly for clarification and go back into small groups for suggesting more ideas that might have been generated by sharing information. From this exercise there may be many ways the group can go to expand and refine ideas: stay in small groups and discuss ideas, selecting the craziest, most practical, we've done them before and other categories to present to the group. Have the large group again discuss ideas and conduct a discussion session on what is crazy but workable if we change this or that. There are many ways the groups can go with brainstormed ideas depending upon their overall goal.

and work to that point. For example, during a recent session we facilitated, a group agreed to meet monthly and at different locations within the state. Some members of the group said that they would not be able to attend all meetings but they supported meeting in other locations as an appropriate mechanism to generate visibility for the group. Two members of the group attended only one of the early meetings then skipped four meetings and came into the last meeting with a new agenda and a deliberate attempt to restructure recommendations that had been discussed thoroughly and worked out in meetings two, three, four, and five. Minutes of all meetings had been prepared and mailed to the all group members so they would have a record of the discussions, decisions, and recommendations. As the absentees became more vocal, tried to "re-discuss," and lobbied for changing the agreed-upon recommendations the group resisted their efforts more and more strongly. Finally, one of the group members bluntly said, "We have had these discussions before! If you had attended meetings two, three, four, and five you would have been able to take part in the decisions. We are ready to move on to other issues!" In this situation the group enforced its own participation opportunity rules. Everyone had the opportunity to participate. Furthermore, if members did participate they could have influenced decisions. By choosing not to participate they had to live with the group's results! The group was insulted by the absentees' tactics to change the agenda and successfully resisted their efforts to change their results.

SUMMARY

Facilitators have many tasks to perform and their skills will be challenged when managing various activities in the meeting. Starting the meeting off on the right foot is critical but so is running the meeting. Knowing when to change directions based upon the group's needs and being flexible enough to accommodate members wanting to evaluate or critique ideas too soon will test the facilitators' egos and their group process skills.

CHAPTER 6

Consensus Building and Collaborating on Problem Solving

Each day people are faced with situations, problems, and decisions to be made. Communities have an agglomeration of these issues to be addressed and resolved in a timely fashion. In many instances full-time or part-time city or county officials handle these problems. However, more emphasis is being placed on decentralizing decision making. This requires utilizing a wider range of citizens in problem-solving and decision-making processes. Birkey (1984) suggests that as problems become more complex there is a need for citizens and officials to have more experience and training in problem-solving approaches.

PROBLEM-SOLVING PROCESS

Successful problem solving requires that the individual or group attend to the stages or steps in a process. Specific skills and experience are needed in defining the problem, thinking up, and developing ideas for possible solutions, evaluating solutions, and designing plans of action. The group problem-solving process flow, discussed in this section describes how we have facilitated groups through problem-solving approaches. Figure 6.1 shows the steps in such a process.

Facilitators are managers of group discussion and creativity, working toward a level of agreement or acceptance of alternatives for problem solving and decision making. Agreement is reached through discussion of issues, needs, barriers, and possible solutions. More, rather than less, input, ideas, or options are

ACTION	GROUP TASK	BARRIERS	PROCESSES
Define the problem(s)	Problem clarification	Jump to solutions Don't understand problem	Two words for problem, problem picture (visual), needs analysis
Discuss/verify problem	Discussion	Critique to soon Introduce solutions	NGT/words to describe problem(s)
Critique/Analyze problem(s)	Build Criteria	Don't apply same criteria to all problems	NGT Strength/Weakness analysis; sticking dots to select problem(s)
Solution(s) for Problem(s)	Opinions about what will solve problem	Automatic assignment of solution to problem	Brainstorm options Brainwrite and post on the walls
Discuss Possible Solutions	Potentials and Liabilities of Solutions	"Nay Sayers" not willing to dream	Draw/illustrate new designs
Select "best" solution or option	Achieve consensus on decision	Not willing to collaborate or work toward consensus	Sticking Dots, Lobby and Select
Put option into action	Design Action Plan	No Commitment to Action	Action Plans, Selecting What you can/want to do
Response to action	Evaluation Assessment	Bias toward success/failure	Application of criteria to results

Figure 6.1   *Group problem-solving process flow*

solicited from the group. Diverse opinions, conflicting views, and personal agendas are exposed to get as much variation on the table as the group can tolerate. The facilitator manages this variation in a structured process such as suspending evaluation of ideas, building upon ideas with brainwriting or similar techniques, and then tries to get a sense of support for options by using some technique to quickly see where interests converge. Voting or win-lose techniques are held off as last resort processes. Small and large group discussions about alternatives, options, and new ideas are used to get more participation and eventually ownership of priorities and potential solutions which the group will implement. These are some of the strategies that facilitators use to achieve consensus, not unanimous but general agreement, to support an idea, option, or solution.

Several months ago we (our organization) were asked by a

local official to work with a group concerning an issue, local recreation programming. The design dance indicated that local officials were being criticized by citizens regarding the lack of recreation facilities. For example, complaints included not enough picnic tables at parks, need for separate jogging and bike trails, no special facilities for senior citizens at park sites, playground areas dominated by one sport to the exclusion of other interests, and not enough supervision for youth. From interviews, observations, and volunteered information the lead facilitator determined that local officials wanted someone or some agency to meet with the irate citizens and catch the flak. And in the view of local officials, because there was so much animosity in the group it would be impossible to reach consensus. Therefore, the facilitators would be blamed for the lack of progress and the "heat" would be off of the county officials. Knowing this from the start in the design dance and even anticipating a tough session, the lead facilitator still agreed to conduct the session.

Some design decisions were made immediately by the facilitators. First, to allow group members to wear their hats and express their irritation about lack of recreation facilities, programming, and other issues. Second, to openly lay these feelings on the table early in the session without personal attacks toward officials or others. Third, to focus group attention on the problem and channel group energy into problem clarification and possible options for addressing the problem.

It was a tough session! Right away facilitators constantly had to remind the group of the ground rules (that is, no personal attacks and no evaluation or critique of ideas at this time). In the afternoon session of the first day, the group realized: (1) what it could do; and, (2) what it must do for recreation in the community. The group had been asked for recommendations by local officials and members could not get to these issues if they continued to squabble and fight with each other. They needed to work together. And they did just that, worked together, with an occasional "violation of the ground rules" and complaints about " . . . how hard it was to work with people in the group that they didn't know personally but had heard rumors about." They demonstrated a determination that they " . . . would show the local officials that the group could work together!" Consensus was reached on items that previously could not be spoken about in recreation meetings (for example, multiple group use of ball fields and scheduling of facilities by many groups rather than only by the power clique group) for fear of verbal and physical abuse. This zero-history group emerged as a powerful ad hoc group that was able to influence local officials to improve recreation facilities. Also, for better or worse, one of the local recreation officials, who had been identified in the interviews as a contributor to the lack of communication and poor maintenance of facilities, was fired. The intent of the group was to find a replacement for this person who could communicate with and work with a diverse set of recreation interests.

Consensus in this situation was achieved, not by the facilitator but, by the group adhering to a meeting process. The group participants developed the process which included airing their feelings, suspending judgment until appropriate, discussing conflicting views, and working toward a level of agreement on the general problem which was to improve poorly designed and maintained recreation facilities for all citizens and recreation interests in the community.

ASSISTING GROUPS WITH PROBLEM-SOLVING STEPS

The facilitator is neutral to the agenda but aggressive toward the process! This has been said before, but it deserves repeating in this section. The facilitator is aggressive about forcing the group to address each of the steps or stages in a problem-solving process. He or she proposes a particular group process or exercise that is designed to optimize the group's energy for dealing with that step in the problem-solving process.

Many different authorities have laid out problem-solving approaches (for example, Dimock, 1987; Adams, 1979; Gordon,

1961). Almost all of these approaches to problem solving involve a series of steps such as:

- defining the problem,
- analysis of the problem,
- generation of problem solutions,
- selecting a probable or best solution, and
- reviewing the results.

In recent years the strict assumption of a linear approach to problem solving has been criticized for not reflecting *real-world* and *real-time* conditions. It has been noted that individuals and groups most often do not start with the first step and move sequentially through each step. Instead, people go back to earlier steps as new information is made available. Earlier assumptions are questioned and changed. So rather than a linear approach, actual problem solving involves the steps noted above but they are pursued in a cyclical manner. Whorton (1993) indicates how a cyclical approach to problem solving has been used in facilitated sessions to foster the development of effective community groups.

A real-time, real-world approach would be to include in a facilitated session, those individuals who:

- helped create the problem,
- are recipients of the problem,
- are impacted by the problem,
- are managers of the problem,
- must implement possible solutions to the problem, and
- are otherwise associated with the problem.

In this situation, the expert problem solvers are not seated at the discussion table to dominate, because of their knowledge. They are brought to the group to respond to specific requests for information or to interpret the data. Problem solving in this context becomes the domain of those associated with the problem and those who must implement possible solutions. However, expert opinion can be helpful in this effort.

Group attendees are those people more closely associated with the issues such as community members concerned about ways to provide for more local economic development. People involved in a recent community economic development problem-solving session included: county commissioners, business owners, homeowners, community leaders, state legislative representatives, chamber of commerce members, two high school students, environmentalists, transportation directors, members of the town council, and economic development experts.

An Example Group Using a
Problem-Solving Process Flow

A group we facilitated recently used the group problem-solving process illustrated in Figure 6.1. This zero-history group began with introductions of each other in pairs, introduced facilitators, agreed that the two-day meeting was held to examine options for promoting economic development, generated ideas about the problem, met in small groups to discuss the problem, reached consensus in the large group, and used sticking dots (see Example 6.1) to select four issues that needed to be addressed to help solve economic development concerns in the area. Following this discussion the group brainstormed in small and large groups, about how these four issues could be resolved. Several economic development options were identified. The group expressed concern that some of the options could be accomplished by a phone call from the appropriate leader or public official, whereas other options would need extensive work. The group members were instructed to walk up to the flip charts and mark (with sticking dots, see Example 6.1) the three ideas that they thought needed to be worked on before attempting other strategies. Once these options were identified (that is, items receiving the most sticking dots) the group began the design of an action plan to achieve these options. The meeting closed with developing an action plan and seeking volunteers to be responsible for parts of the plan.

Example 6.1 *Sticking Dots*

"This technique is one of the simplest and most efficient methods available. Members each receive a fixed number of self-sticking dots with which they can indicate their preferences with minimal time and effort" (VanGundy, 1984, p. 209).

We have used this technique with groups to get a quick indication of members' preference for discussing issues. Following possible discussion of criteria for selecting issues, members are given several dots (fewer than 20% of the total issues) which they can allocate among the topics as they wish. They cannot cut dots in halves or quarters. Following the placing of dots on issues listed on paper around the meeting room, we discuss those issues that did not receive dots, those that received a few and those that received the most dots. We conclude with an indication from the members that they want to discuss X, Y, and Z issues.

Frequently, when using sticking dots some group members will hurry to place their dots while others wait, watch, and then place their dots, sometimes on topics that others have avoided. It is essential to review and facilitate a discussion of what was revealed by the dots.

Attending to the Process Steps

Individuals working in groups tend to want to jump to the solution first. In Western culture we pride ourselves in being practical, efficient, and able to solve problems fast. Sometimes we want the solution before we even fully understand the problem. Even worse, we often have a favorite solution and want to apply it no matter what the problem is! One of the strategies for community groups is to invest time, lots of time, maybe more time than the group wants to invest, in discussing what the issues or problems are. This ensures that groups better understand the problems or issues involved and that they link up the solutions to the right problem (Volkema, 1983).

As groups engage in generating alternatives, they frequently want to evaluate ideas as they are offered. If they engage in a concurrent critique they will stifle members' creativity. People will fear sharing ideas that they know will be attacked. You must specifically help them to delay evaluating ideas until the generate step is complete. There are many techniques which are helpful in getting groups to identify issues and then begin to creatively generate possible solutions. We have included descriptions of how we use brainwriting, brainstorming, and the nominal group technique (NGT) in detail in chapters four and five (see Figure 4.1, Example 5.4, and Example 4.2 respectively). These are not the only techniques we use and we suggest consulting resources such as VanGundy (1984, 1988), University Associates Handbooks for Facilitators (1972–1991) and Delbecq, Van de Ven & Gustafson (1975).

You need to be flexible to help groups cycle back and forth among the steps in the problem-solving process. But you must also help them to respect the importance of each step of the process. Do not let them skip a step, for example, defining the problem. Do not let them compromise one step by prematurely moving into another step. As facilitator you must attend to the appropriate task in each step.

SUMMARY

Most of the work we do with community and decision-making groups is to gain consensus about which issues need to be addressed and what are the appropriate, in the group's point of view, strategies for solution and action. Accommodating different points of view while working toward a solution, which the group can really get behind and support, is one of the primary goals of facilitated problem solving.

CHAPTER 7

Helping Groups Identify and Explore Expectations and Issues

Once the group has agreed upon, modified, and specified ground rules about how to operate and conduct business within the meeting, we usually follow with a discussion of expectations about what each person wants from this meeting. Questions which usually begin this part of the session, that cue the group as to what the facilitator is trying to accomplish, might be:

- What has to happen this morning (or today or over the next two days) for this meeting to be a success?
- What one thing has to happen at this meeting for it be useful to you?

Specifically, the facilitator directs each member to answer these, or questions like these, individually and then to share responses with the group for consideration. As the group begins the expectations exercise it may be appropriate to review the ground rules, particularly as they relate to individuals: not criticizing items mentioned by group members, not giving more than one item at a time, not allowing participants to dominate or change the process, or not assuming the role of expert when the procedure requires all participants to express their views.

EXPECTATIONS OF THE GROUP

As members present ideas, concerns and "must dos," the facilitator lists these items without allowing critique or comment by the group. After all items have been listed the group may want to ask individual members for clarification and then they may want to discuss them at length in small groups before using this information as a basis for selecting topics for the meeting.

As the meeting progresses from morning session to afternoon session or to the second day, the facilitator may want to explicitly ask the group to confirm that it is making progress toward achieving its goals. If group members confirm that they are progressing as planned, then proceed to work on the topics identified previously. If they indicate that they would like to revise the initial list of topics, check this concern with the entire group for consensus about changing or revising their subjects and proceed in the direction indicated.

Facilitators have several options once groups have identified their expectations, which could be items or actions they would like to accomplish at the community meeting. One option is to look at the topics generated by the group, see if there are overlapping or similar items that might form a cluster or category, and then have the group set a priority ordering for discussing the items. Expectations identified at a recent facilitator skills training session we conducted (see Example 7.1) illustrates participants' interest in discussing a variety of topics related to facilitation.

Participants were instructed to review the list to look for clusters, commonalty among items, and categories of concerns. Participants grouped these individual items into larger categories for discussion. Example 7.2 displays the clustering of expectations into five categories related to facilitation. Following this discussion we then asked the group to select one category, by using sticking dots (see Example 6.1), to begin the morning's discussion and training session about facilitation skills.

In the previous example, participants attending a meeting about " . . . becoming a better facilitator" had specific items they wanted discussed. They had developed ideas and specific things they expected to learn about during the meeting. If they did not discuss these topics, then for them the meeting would not have been a success.

Example 7.1 *Expectations Identified at a Facilitator Training Session*

Twenty eight items were listed by 10 participants at a facilitator training session. These were items participants indicated that they hoped to have addressed during the session. Items are listed and numbered representing the order in which they were mentioned during a nominal group technique, round robin reporting.

1. When do you be more directive? How far do you let groups go?
2. How do you manage conflict?
3. How can you use facilitation techniques in teaching (graduate and undergraduate students)?
4. How can you manage the process when the facilitator has a strong view?
4a. How do you resolve a conflict when the facilitator has trouble being objective?
5. How can you plan effective meetings?
6. How can you communicate technical information?
7. How do you manage a blocker?
8. How do you identify internal stress (hidden) among members?
9. How do you size up group dynamics and change original plans?
10. How can you deal with a stonewall group?
11. How can you set up expectations to maximize goals and objectives?
12. How should you facilitate when you are knowledgeable versus when you are not? What are the differences?
13. How do you negotiate ground rules/contracts?
14. How do you handle challenges from the group of the facilitator's credibility?
15. How can you keep a group on topic?
16. How do you know when you're done?
17. How does a chairperson facilitate the group?
18. How much do you reveal to group about the facilitator, process, and agenda?
19. What powers do facilitators have? What is the proper use of those powers?
20. What should you do if the facilitator discovers he or she *is* an expert on the topic?
21. How can you deal with two group members who argue?

22. If the facilitator *knows* the solution will not work, what should he or she do?
23. What format should you use?
24. What special things might be done when facilitating groups with cultural diversity?
25. How do you determine the kind of help needed by a group?
26. Are there rules for the expert, recorder, and facilitator?
27. How detailed or specific should you be with ground rules?

Informing the Group

We use the expectations exercise to inform facilitators and group members about what needs to be done for a particular group. We also use this exercise to communicate with the group what we are prepared to do today, tonight, tomorrow, and by follow-up activity. In some instances it is not possible to meet all expectations and we discuss this with the group. From this discussion we identify alternatives that can be accomplished to meet expectations. The list may also reveal that one or a few people have inappropriate or divergent expectations. This can be dealt with at the beginning of the session, rather than waiting to discover the problem at the end of the meeting.

Once the expectations items are listed, ask the group to review the list and look for gaps and overlapping ideas or activities. Can the list be grouped to form categories of information or activities? Let the group suggest the categories and items to be included in each category. It may be necessary during the categorizing/grouping process to ask someone to explain an idea or concept. It is important at this point not to allow the group to get into criticizing, but to focus on only clarifying items so they can be clustered for further discussion.

Keeping the expectations list and agenda visible for all the group to see during the meeting is a powerful communication technique. It says to the group, if we are not on the right subject (the topics you specified that must be discussed) tell us. After a topic is discussed, clarified, and decided, it can be crossed off or marked as having been accomplished. This reinforces to the

Example 7.2 *Categorizing/Grouping the Expectations List*

At a training session on facilitating in community settings, participants first listed 28 specific things they *expected* to discuss during the training (as reported in Example 7.1). These were then reviewed and grouped by the participants into five headings, with only one item, item number 4a, placed into two categories. Reported here are the five categories and the items listed within category in the order placed there by the group at the time of the categorizing.

SKILLS AND APPLICATIONS, ETC.

3. How can you use facilitation techniques in teaching (graduate and undergraduate students)?
24. What special things might be done when facilitating groups with cultural diversity?
6. How can you communicate technical information?
12. How should you facilitate when you are knowledgeable versus when you are not? What are the differences?
18. How much do you reveal to group about the facilitator, process, and agenda?
26. Are there relative rules for the expert, recorder, and facilitator?

LOGISTICS AND SETUP

5. How can you plan effective meetings?
13. How do you negotiate ground rules/contracts?
25. How do you determine the kind of help needed by a group?
23. What format should you use?
27. How detailed or specific should you be with ground rules?

CONFLICT

2. How do you manage conflict?
4a.* How do you resolve a conflict when facilitator has trouble being objective?
7. How do you manage a blocker?
8. How do you identify internal stress (hidden) among members?
21. How can you deal with two group members who argue?
14. How do you handle challenges from the group of the facilitator's credibility?

ETHICAL ISSUES

4. How can you manage the process when the facilitator has a strong view?
19. What powers do facilitators have? What is the proper use of those powers?
17. How does a chairperson facilitate the group?
22. If the facilitator *knows* the solution will not work, what should he or she do?
20. What should you do if the facilitator discovers he or she *is* an expert on the topic?
4a.* How do you resolve a conflict when facilitator has trouble being objective?

GROUP PROCESS

1. When do you be more directive? How far do you let groups go?
9. How do you size up group dynamics and chance original plans?
10. How can you deal with a stonewall group?
11. How can you set up expectations to maximize goals and objectives?
16. How do you know when you're done?
15. How can you keep a group on topic?

group that it is making progress toward its goals or intended purpose. Keeping the expectations list visible can also be used to "check in" periodically with the group as they work toward their specific goals and they can use this tool as a mechanism to keep themselves on track.

Whose Items Are on the List?

If an item doesn't make it to the expectations list who is responsible? It must be clearly understood that it is the individual member's responsibility for getting his or her items on the list. It's their agenda! It's their responsibility to take part. If the rule is to state the items publicly, enforce the rule. Do not allow a group member to whisper to you an item to add to the list. It's the facilitator's responsibility to provide multiple opportunities for members to express their ideas and concerns, but members must speak out!

Even after all members have indicated their *must do* or *must consider* items, the facilitator can ask for additional points which may have come to mind during the listing of expectations. This has the potential for being a very long session but, in actual practice group members seem to appreciate the opportunity to add one or two more items. It demonstrates the commitment to openness and inclusiveness.

If the group is sensitive toward a topic or if the facilitator senses a reluctance to raise a topic in the group he or she may want to use sheets of letter sized paper on which members write their ideas and drop them in a central repository. The facilitator can call a break for the group and use this time to gather the papers, redistribute them to group members, or post them to the wall. The facilitator should watch for occasions when the group wants to be able to express ideas anonymously.

Deviations from Expectations

When does the facilitator deviate from the group's expectations or agenda? Never on his or her own, without first checking with the group. Expectations may be revisited by individual members and the facilitator at any point during the meeting. However, it is common practice to check with the group periodically during the meeting, after breaks, after meals, beginning of the next day, and whenever the group requests, to confirm that the meeting is progressing appropriately. Sometimes it may be helpful to the facilitator to get an idea of which items the group would like to address next. In this situation, using sticking dots (see Example 6.1 adapted from VanGundy, 1984) may provide a quick indication of the importance and priority of an item by the group. Give all people in the group one, two, three, or four colored sticking dots (about the size of a penny) to place on one or more items they would like to discuss in the next session. Make clear that they cannot cut dots in half; they must use a whole dot for each item; they can use all dots on a single item or in various combinations. The result will be a visual presentation of how the group feels about what should be considered next in the discussion. Other effective polling techniques can also obtain quick and explicit assessments from the group.

ISSUES FOR THE MEETING

Asking groups about their expectations will not always generate a list of issues that they wish to address. Sometimes when we begin a group session we ask a general question about expectations that serves as an icebreaker exercise. For example, asking group members to write a headline for an article in the local newspaper about the meeting allows participants to creatively state what they hope to accomplish. Such an exercise will typically lead to general statements about the different elements coalescing into a group with a unified vision. This type of exercise will usually not lead to a specific listing of topics that need to be addressed in the current group session. Therefore, if the expectations exercise has resulted in a set of general and aspirational statements, either by conscious design or by chance, the group can be asked to list the specific issues to be discussed at the session.

In some instances with a community group we ask participants to identify local issues or problems. For example, individuals may have been asked to attend a meeting about a particular topic such as developing a recreation plan for the community or discussing problems with locating a solid waste site in our county. In this situation the invitation letter has identified the issue and people attend the meeting with certain ideas and feelings about the issue. We use these normal and natural feelings of individuals to identify issues for an agenda.

After ground rules have been discussed and accepted by the group and after expectations have been explored, you may want to start the issues identification process by reviewing the invitation letter, such as:

• you were invited to attend a meeting to decide about the need for a community recreation plan, or

- you were invited to participate in a meeting about locating a solid waste site in our area.

If one of these or other similar statements were in the letter, ask the attendees what they think we ought to discuss today, this weekend, or at tonight's meeting? This is a very broad question. The facilitator might rephrase it to be, "What do you think has to be done today to decide about the recreation plan or the solid waste site?" A more specific request would be, "What two things have to be done today *by you and the group* for it to be a successful meeting?" Give people a few minutes to think about one of these questions and write their responses on paper or cards. The facilitator has several options at this point. If the issue is really emotional and she or he is concerned that participants may not want to read their own ideas, you might collect all the paper or cards, mix them up and pass them back out to the group to be read anonymously. Following the nominal group technique procedures (see Example 4.1, or VanGundy, 1988), ask each participant to read one item. The facilitator will write each item on white boards or flip chart paper and proceed around the group until all items have been listed.

At a recent meeting we conducted about developing facilitation skills we asked members to list two issues they would like to address during a two-day session. Thirty-five items (see Example 7.3) were identified by the group in the initial brainstorming, NGT exercise; sticking dots were used to select topics for small group discussion; small groups selected two issues for discussion, item #9 (see Example 7.4) and item #12 (see Example 7.5) and generated suggestions for facilitating groups.

By using cuing questions about individual and group issues related to facilitation, participants identified 35 topics. Using sticking dots they reduced the priority items for discussion to 10. Each small group picked 1 of the 10 facilitation issues for discussion and brainstorming and then shared that information with the reassembled large group (see Examples 7.4 and 7.5). As the meeting progressed, the participants discussed all 10 priority issues in small groups and shared the small groups' ideas with the total group.

Example 7.3 *Issues about Facilitation Skills*

Participants at a session first generated this list and then voted for those items on the list that they most wanted to address. The 10 most important items are indicated by a dot. Small groups addressed these items. Group ideas for issues 9 and 12 and are included in later figures to illustrate key points about the discussion.

ISSUES: What things about facilitation would you most like to discuss during the session?

1. How to use facilitation techniques to improve the education of groups.
2. To develop a feeling of self-confidence about one's facilitation skills.
3. How to be facilitated (to be a better participant in facilitated sessions).
4. To better understand what is available (techniques, tools, approaches) to bring together community leaders to build a common agenda.
5. How to capture on the flip charts what a person has said (given that it may be a rambling statement).
• 6. How to work with a community group to set goals for which it will feel ownership.
7. A set of principal do's and don'ts.
8. How to get a group to accept change—how to handle negative views of change.
• 9. Ways to control or direct participants who engage in one-on-one dialogues or argument.
10. Learn how to better provide technical information to a group—how to get it to better digest an oral presentation.
11. To learn how to manipulate a group.
• 12. How to get people to participate and open up.
13. Ideas or techniques to use for specific situations.
• 14. How to deal with participants who dominate or monopolize the sessions.
15. How to diffuse controversial situations—how not to get pulled into the controversy.
16. How to ensure good follow-up.
17. How to keep on schedule without being rude [or how to build realistic schedules].
18. Icebreakers.

- 19. Good techniques to make sure that you have their attention from the start.
  20. How to build consensus.
  21. How to keep the group from turning against you.
- 22. How to keep the group focused.
  23. When to act as facilitator versus expert.
  24. How to get group members to ask themselves the right question or the right basic questions.
  25. How to legitimately "unlock" a group without violating the Star Trek rules not to contaminate a planet's culture.
  26. How to get the group to understand the process and trust the process.
- 27. What to do when "some are more equal than others"—when there are superiors and subordinates, and so on.
  28. What facilitation is.
  29. How to recognize the need. Why and when to facilitate.
- 30. How to keep group focused on the agency agenda.
  31. Group dynamics.
- 32. How to help a group to think creatively.
  33. How to deal with someone in the group who is a cynic or a "wise-ass."
  34. How to use dual facilitators or a team to conduct a facilitated session.
  35. How to bring a group together on an agenda or a reduced set of brainstormed ideas.

NOTE: Items that are marked with the • in the margin were addressed in small groups. Suggestions from two of these sessions (#9 and #12) are presented in later examples.

Clarifying Issues

One of the critical tasks for a facilitator working with community groups is to make sure that all members of the group understand the issues being raised within the group. Clarifying issues can be done in a variety of ways from a simple explanation by a group member, to having a group member respond to questions, to a more involved discussion or exercise led by the facili-

94   FACILITATING COMMUNITY DECISION MAKING

Example 7.4   *Ideas Generated by Small Group to Handle Item #9*

ITEM 9: How to keep one-on-one arguments from becoming a problem or how to lessen their disruptiveness.

1. Know participants well enough (via interviews) to be prepared for the kinds of issues that might trigger confrontation.
2. Have the group generate its own ground rules.
3. State the ground rules up front and amplify them if needed.
4. Assert that this is a violation of the ground rules.
5. As part of maintaining the ground rules participants are given the right to "bomb" violators with crumpled paper balls.
6. Reassure participant concerns and then try to redirect the discussion to others in the group.
7. Acknowledge contribution by the participant and move on to another point.
8. Register both opinions before going on; list each point on flip charts.
9. Try to keep others involved if you sense a problem.
10. Acknowledge the emotions: admit this is a hot issue; say, "Let's hear what else is involved."
11. Physically place yourself between the people; posturing as the custodian of the process.
12. Tactfully redirect or change the subject to defuse the situation.
13. Take a break and say when the group gets back, "We'll return to the agenda at hand."
14. Suggest that the two people get together at a break to discuss this point further. Ask group members if they wish to continue with this. Do not lend credibility to the argument.
15. If all else fails, take a break.

tator. A procedure which describes one way the facilitator can engage the group in issue clarification is illustrated in Example 7.6.

SUMMARY

We assume that all people invited to a facilitated meeting have certain expectations they hope to accomplish and they know about specific issues, concerns, or problems that need at-

Example 7.5   *Ideas Generated by Small Group to Handle Item #12*

ITEM 12: How to get people to open up and participate.

1. Conduct a "show and tell" or expectations exercise to get folks talking.
2. Use the nominal group technique (NGT).
3. Include it (NGT) in the ground rules (let it be known that everyone will be called on to participate).
4. Employ fun and games approach with an icebreaker.
5. Indicate that the ideas do not have to be "gems."
6. Allow no negative feedback.
7. Call on specific people.
8. Use the directional approach—say, "We haven't heard from anyone from accounting or from over here."
9. Use the participants' own words as items are written down.
10. Emphasize ownership of final product.
11. Read the body language to identify potential active participants.
12. The facilitator's demeanor: be encouraging, sharing yourself.
13. Give an example to clarify the subject and ensure that it is bite-size.
14. Use "brainwriting" when people are afraid to speak out.
15. Use break-out groups.
16. The facilitator shows his or her own fallibility and gullibility.
17. Use silence. The facilitator is silent. Don't offer suggestions, see what the group recommends.

tention. Identifying and exploring their expectations and issues helps to expand and set the group's agenda for discussion and change. By working with the group to immediately and collectively build the agenda for the session, the facilitator sets the norm for group ownership and control of the topic and results of the session. Finally, while the facilitator can never eliminate hidden agendas, creating the opportunity for participants to state the issues that they believe the group needs to address helps to limit the existence of hidden agendas that can disrupt the group.

Example 7.6 *Issues Clarification*

Describe the situation:

When describing a problem situation people usually grumble about what is happening and what needs to happen without being specific. For example, this community needs more economic development. We need more business and industry moving into the area. Then the "situation" is: we need to attract more industry or business to the community.

Clarify the problem:

Focus attention of the group toward the problem or specific issue. How do we get what we want? What are the conditions that need to be changed or overcome or solved? For example, What needs to be done to attract industry? Are there other ways to create economic development? What needs to be worked on now, next to attract more business or industry?

Specify actions for the future:

As participants move from "grumbling" about what is happening to what needs to happen they can direct their attention to the desired outcome or resolution of the issue. Example: For economic development we can do several things . . . attract new industry, expand existing industry, develop or "home grow" local industries, invest monies for development locally, look at products we buy outside the community or region and buy them locally, and so on.

The process described above moves the group from a point of complaining and grumbling about the situation to one of clarifying issues, identifying options and taking action to meet future needs. In the example about economic development the groups move from complaining about not having business and industry development to accepting responsibility for this situation and taking specific actions to solve this problem.

CHAPTER 8

Closing the Meeting

How do you close the meeting? Stop because it is 5:00 p.m.? Have a closing ceremony? Tell everyone they worked hard (if it is the truth) and say goodbye! We have included several examples of what groups have done at the end of their meetings. Some review their mission statement after working on specific issues and tasks they believe the organization should accomplish. Other groups, depending upon their particular needs, end the meeting by developing and getting commitment to an action plan. They address the next steps for the group after today's meeting. Their attention is toward what should be worked on, changed, or accomplished before meeting again.

MISSION STATEMENT

An organization's mission may be stated as an expression of how to accomplish "what good (or service) for which people and at what cost?" (Carver, 1990, p. 58). When facilitating groups about some community need or improvement, often someone will suggest that the group develop a mission (or goal) statement or begin by rewriting such a statement. Someone will state that the group needs to have a mission statement to know what to decide while planning. Someone will state that the group should start with a mission statement that is a general yet comprehensive summary of the group's purpose and how it functions. Our experience is, and perhaps a more honest statement would be to say that our painful experience is, that groups frequently bog down if they try to begin with a mission statement.

As a general rule we ask the group to consider holding this activity until later in the meeting. At the later point the group is better able to review what it has specified as priority issues, suggested actions for problem solving, or implementation strategies. The group can then attempt to write a mission statement to fit what it has done. Therefore, an alternative for ending the meeting is to develop (or review) a mission statement based upon the problems, issues, and possible actions needed. If this is a zero-history group it may want to formally organize, establish a mission, and use the action plan as it's guide for implementing change in the community.

So, our experience is that groups are better off working from more specific issues and actions toward a mission statement. If a group resists our suggestions to hold off on a mission statement until later, we will try to get the group to limit the discussion of mission to some terse sense of what the organization or group should try to do. We can help the group to get some agreement about what it will do or the limits on the scope of its activities. We are normally insistent about not going further than that. We have two primary reasons for trying to hold off the writing or rewriting of mission statements until the end of the session. First, as stated before, we believe that it is easier to write a general mission statement to fit a set of agreed-upon activities and objectives than it is to first write a good mission statement and then develop the activities, and so on. The second reason to delay a mission statement until late in the session is that people seem to go slightly crazy when trying to write mission statements. For example, you can ask group members not to worry about punctuation or whether to use "that" or "which" as they draft a mission statement and they will all agree that that makes sense. Then they will argue about punctuation and whether to use that or which. Additionally, people seem to feel more possessive about their suggested mission statement than about other ideas that are brainstormed, so there will be hurt feelings as one person's suggestion gets criticized by others. Writing of the mission statement late in the session limits the time that can be spent, lets you build upon the good group dynamics that have developed, and generalizes the decisions that have been made.

ACTION PLANS

It is our bias to work with groups and actually contract for the development of an action plan which the participants produce and can take with them when they leave the meeting. The document or meeting result would then include specific reference to what needs to be done and who is to be responsible for taking the lead or doing the work.

We like to conclude the meeting with a plan of action with individual group members knowing what they want to do next and for what purpose. Action plans are only one approach toward achieving this objective. However, we have found this technique to be very effective in determining the commitment for achieving specific tasks that the group decided were important for improving their community or organization.

Using the Five W's

One approach to developing action plans is to use the five W's; asking for specification of why, who, what, when and where. This stimulates groups to think about:

- Why is this action needed?
- What needs to be done?
- Where should these actions take place?
- When do we take action?
- Who will be responsible for which actions?

Specific questions about developing action plans and the five W's are illustrated in Example 8.1.

Example 8.1   *The 5 W's*

WHY?

- Why is this plan needed?
- Why hasn't someone else (individual or group) solved the problem?
- Why does this group need to be concerned?
- Why should we (group members) take action?
- Why not involve more people and groups in the community?

WHAT?

- What needs to be done to correct the problem or change the situation?
- What are the logical first steps to solving the problem?
- What can be done in a short time span (3–6 months); long term (1–2 years)?
- What is our (group members') responsibility?
- What community groups do we need to keep informed of our actions?
- What other groups or individuals do we need to help implement the plan?
- What will be the roles and responsibilities of these additional members or groups?

WHERE?

- Where should these actions take place?
- Where can we make the most impact with the time and resources available?
- Where do we report our problems, successes?
- Where do we go from here?
- Where do we receive information, suggestions, and recommendations from others in the community?
- Where do we locate resources to apply to the action plan?
- Where do we hold public meetings about programs toward completing the plan?

WHEN?

- When do we take action?
- When do we involve the group?
- When do we contact key leaders in the community?
- When do we report to the group or community?

- When do we need to reach key milestones?
- When do we add new members and organizations to the group?

WHO?
- Who will take the lead on some or all of the actions?
- Who will be responsible for which actions?
- Who will be "in charge" of coordinating individual and small group activities?
- Who reports to the news media?
- Who will call the group back together to discuss actions and needs?

Structuring Action Plans

Action plans can organize ideas about group projects in formats such as shown in Figure 8.1. Copies of a form with this outline were given to a group. The group had several activities it wanted accomplished but didn't have a good idea about what to do next. Working in small groups people identified a program area and tried to specify the objectives, action steps, who would be the leader, what would be the time frame, and what resources would be required. Also, they were able to identify key participants and the assumptions and/or relationships necessary for achieving their objectives. This tool helped direct ideas and program needs into a manageable plan of action.

Responsibility for Actions

In some instances it may be desirable to assign activities to individuals and small groups. However, in the spirit of facilitation, we believe it advisable for individuals in the group to volunteer for all or parts of an action. The cuing questions could be:

- Can any individual or small group take responsibility for doing this item (on the "to do" plan list)?
- You may not be able to do everything . . . but can you help the

Major Program Area:

Programmatic Objectives:

CRITICAL ACTION STEPS	LEADERSHIP ROLE	TIME FRAME	CRITICAL RESOURCES NEEDED
1)			
2)			
3)			

Key Participants:

Critical Assumptions/Relationships:

Figure 8.1 *Form for developing initial set of action assignments*

group get started by doing one or more steps related to a particular item?

The facilitator would write down the individual (committee, or small group) who is volunteering to take responsibility for a specific action. See Figure 8.2, Action Plans, for an illustration of how issues, actions needed, key players, first steps, and timetable and policy champions were organized from a recent facilitated two-day meeting about community economic development. Four issues were identified in the group work session. Some group discussion produced information about the actions needed. Cuing questions for the group were:

• What needs to happen for the group to resolve each issue?
• Who are the key players in these decisions?

- What are the first, next, and concluding steps to resolve the issue?
- What is the timetable and who will work on the issue?

In some instances our facilitation of a group as it attempts to deal with action plans focuses on other ways to identify who will have responsibility for follow-through or actions. In some cases when we have worked with the board of directors of an organization we have provided time for a final set of small group work sessions. In this last small group session the participants have been asked to assemble by their usual committee structure and consider which committees would have primary and secondary responsibility for accomplishing the tasks that had already been identified as priorities. In cases where the attendees have been representatives of many different community agencies we have asked them to identify the policy champion for the priority items that have been developed. These policy champions are not expected to be personally responsible for full implementation of the ideas. Rather, the champion is asked to serve as the person who speaks for the idea, tries to marshall resources to accomplish the idea, and seeks to build motivation and excitement among people and groups to support and work for the idea. The goal is to leave the meeting with at least one person or organization linked to each priority item and with an agreement that the person or organization will champion the idea.

SUMMARY

The one expectation we carry into a meeting or session that we facilitate is that the group will leave the session with a clear idea of what it needs to accomplish next—in 3 or 6 or 12 months—an action plan. We discuss this expectation in the design dance as one of the things we can help the group work toward. Facilitators need to attend to the timing of the meeting so that the closing activities can address action plans and assignment of follow-up responsibilities. We do not set expectations for ourselves about the content or issues of the group.

Issue	Action(s) Needed	Key Players	First Steps	Timetable and Policy Champions
Development of the Lake Shoreline	The lake is currently restricted for private use and offers a great potential for economic development. The goal is to obtain approval for a 20–30% usage pattern of the lake.	• Corp of Engineers (Undersecretary of the Army) • Congressmen • Lake Authority • County Commissioners • City Council • Environmentalists • Landowners • Governor's Office • Department of Natural Resources • Hotel/motel owners • Business community • Chamber of Commerce	*Overall* • Identify previous commitments (hidden agendas) if any exist. Local leadership effort is important • Lake committee of Chamber should meet with the Lake Authority to discuss the issue and address a community perception of "greed" (who will make the money?), so all can benefit • Form a Lake Development Association • Assess economic impact and other factors that make this an issue affecting the county *Specific Action Steps:* 1. Lake committee of the Chamber will meet and discuss issues of public support for private use of the resource—after delivery of a needs assessment report, in five months. The issues for	The Lake Authority and the Committee of the Chamber will meet to develop a plan of action after the needs assessment report is delivered in five months.

Figure 8.2 *Action plans*

			this group to deal with are: a. Identify the benefits/costs for the community, different groups (those with interest in development), and how to involve these groups b. Identify previous commitments that have not been fulfilled by Corps with the community—interview key individuals c. Form a support group in the community: The Lake Development Association. 1. Create a list of names of people to be on the Council 2. Hold an organizational meeting 3. Find leaders for the Council (Chairman, etc.) 4. Use Chamber Hwy Committee as nucleus for first organizational meeting 5. Conduct promotional and educational efforts *Resources Needed* –The highway plan –Members of the highway committees	–Existing Hwy Committee of the Chamber can start the organizational effort— They will discuss this idea next month.
Four-Lane Council	Create a Four-Lane Council which would serve as an educational, information sharing, and lobbying organization for the completion of key highways. It may be possible to start this effort by using the existing Highway Committee of	• Cities and County government • Existing Highway Committee of the Chamber • Citizens—get involved • Business owners and Mainstreet • Affected landowners • State elected officials • Congressional representatives—Obtain commitment of the candidate • Civic groups		

Issue	Action(s) Needed	Key Players	First Steps	Timetable and Policy Champions
	the Chamber as a catalyst.		−Find $ for mailings, meetings, educational, and promotional efforts −Possibly tap into selling memberships or tapping into the local tax base	
Ensure Quality Growth Along The New Four-Lane Corridors	−Begin to visualize and plan the County with these highways −plan for the development which will take place −Come up with some sort of visual scheme to show how things will look −Goal is to allow for development that is visually appealing and not destructive to	Same as above	1. Find out what ordinances are on the books and what is possible/feasible (zoning ordinances as well) 2. Maintain positive relationships with existing businesses about hwy expansion 3. Hold informational meetings to show people what will be happening—dig out the maps 4. Work together with four-lane highway committees' completion efforts—do not compete	The Four-Lane Council will also address this issue. Chamber President will make sure that the initial meeting takes place. The Highway Committee will get together the week of the 21st for both issues.

Figure 8.2 *Action plans (continued)*

| City/County Economic Development Coordinator | • The people of the County need to convince key players and the general public of the need for a city-county co-ordinator for industrial recruitment, retention of existing business, and coordination of other development activities for all three governments. The immediate need is to gain the approval of the Commission to examine the feasibility of this position/office. | the quality of life that the community wants to preserve. | • Cities
• County
• Chamber of Commerce— to take the initiative | 1. The Chamber President could introduce the concept to the three governing bodies at the next joint government meeting
2. If Commissioners agree to go ahead and study the issue, each government will appoint people to serve on joint committee to develop a proposal
3. Work to gain public support for the person/office
4. Hold organizational meeting to discuss feasibility
5. Be ready to hire in 18 months if resources can be made available. | Chamber President and the large municipality's city manager will begin discussions on how to present this idea to the Commission. If a reasonable plan can be worked out, the Chamber President will present the idea at the next Commission meeting. |

Part III

The After Phase
or What You Do After
You Thought You Were Done

After the group work session ends and the members leave, you can breath a sigh of relief, think about all the things that went well and the things that you wish had gone differently, and start to pack. The packing will include all the equipment you brought and any flip charts, notes, and other data generated at the session. Once things are packed away you can begin the trip home. If a team of you have worked on the project, the travel time back to the office is a great opportunity to do some debriefing. You can share your perceptions about how the meeting went, how your facilitation came across, what else you might have tried, and so on. If you worked alone, you can still use the time to reflect on how things went.

You can also use the time to think about what comes next for the client—because the job is not yet over. The facilitator needs to:

- fulfill obligations regarding a report of the client group's work session,
- address the issue of follow-through and how he or she might productively assist the client in implementation, and
- successfully disengage from the client group.

CHAPTER 9

The Report and Follow-Up

After you complete the facilitated session you still need to ensure that there is some documentation of what happened. Additionally, you need to clarify what follow-up or ongoing support you might provide the client.

REPORTING GROUPS' ACCOMPLISHMENTS

Some consultants are in the business of writing reports. They are product oriented and the product is the report. This report, the product written for the client, typically contains certain information that the consultant has collected and the consultant's expert evaluation or judgment. These types of reports can be found all over the country, on the shelves of managers, elected officials, appointed official, and so on. Too often these reports sit on those shelves and gather dust; years may pass before anything is done or the time is right. These reports sometimes explain the rationale for a predetermined course of action. In some professional fields a major concern is how to get the decision makers to pay more attention to the analyses and the reports. For example, policy analysts frequently lament the seeming lack of impact they and their work have on public policy makers.

As facilitators we are engaged in a different sort of undertaking from these consultants described above. We are not product-oriented consultants; we are process-oriented consultants. Our expertise is in group process, the decision-making process, the problem-solving process, the process! Some facilitators have specifically come to a process-oriented approach because of their frustrations with the report as product-oriented consultant approach sketched out above. The argument implicit in this book has been that a process consultation and facilitation are better ways to help clients come to a better understanding of their problems, invent suitable solutions, and bridge the chasm to greater chances for implementation. Why then does this book even mention reports? Why would a facilitator bother to write a report for a client? What useful purpose does the report possibly serve?

Purposes Served by Reports

One of the more important reasons for the facilitator to generate a report for the client is so that the client group members can focus on what is going on at the work session. The intent is to have them participate fully rather than wildly taking notes. At the start of the group work session the participants can be informed that a report will be created and that certain individuals on the facilitation team are responsible for keeping the record of what happens. Everyone else can be asked to let go of the secretarial function. (Recognize that some people love to take notes and will do so even though they do not have to.)

The report also serves a historical purpose. The report is **the** definitive record of what happened at the meeting. When a question comes up a few weeks or months later, the report can be consulted to see if there is an answer. To the extent that the full brainstormed lists are reported in appendixes or provided as a separate supplement, the report can also serve as a rich source for new ideas about what might be done. The report ensures that nothing has been lost and that all the ideas and work of the group have been archived. Often some good ideas are generated in brainstorming sessions but they were not pursued at that time. Circumstances change, priorities shift, success on one decision allows other avenues to be pursued. The reported brainstormed ideas can be a valuable vein of ore to be mined by the client at later times.

We, as members of an organization, have been the participants in some facilitated sessions at which an outsider was
brought in to facilitate. These were rather productive sessions
and we wrestled with major issues. The facilitator did not, however, generate a report for us. Six months later we could not
remember the conclusions that we had reached or the priorities
that had been set. We are not particularly stupid or forgetful
people. It is simply difficult to remember half a year later what
was done in a meeting without a report. A report allows the client
group members to go back and have their memories jogged.

We have not been able to get away from writing reports.
Often they seem the bane of our existence. We continue to try
to find ways of generating short reports. We use table formats
to display information. We create what we call compilations of
the small and large group work sessions rather than calling them
reports. By calling it a compilation we can write up the lists of
ideas and the list of priorities without inserting a great deal of
verbiage and fluff. We try all sorts of methods. We cannot get
away from writing some kind of report because, ultimately, it
serves a variety of purposes for clients, including:

- specifying the meeting purpose and progress toward accomplishing the objectives;
- providing a record of decision making;
- identifying who participated in the meeting;
- serving as a repository for ideas brainstormed by participants;
- distinguishing among issues, problems, decisions, and actions;
- identifying problems not addressed or left unsolved; and
- suggesting next steps and action plans for the group.

Options for the Report

One thing we are very clear about is that the report ought
not to be a set of minutes of the meeting. The reports that we
produce and that we envision are not verbatim transcripts of
everything that was said and done. The reports do not detail who

said what or attribute remarks or ideas to particular individuals or groups. Because we do not use Robert's Rules of Order, the reports do not indicate who made a motion, who seconded, and the results of a vote. The report is a means for communicating the content of the meeting, the ideas that were generated, the decisions that were reached, and the actions to which attendees committed themselves.

There is no standard report that is written for every client. There is not even a standard format. One issue that should be addressed in the design dance with the client (although we have left it until here to bring up) is what sort of report is to be produced. Along with all of the other possible variations, we typically offer a range of report options from the Cadillac or Mercedes versions down to the used Chevrolet version and even down to the rickshaw versions. Needless to say we attempt to tie the fee charged for services to the length of time that we will have to spend on generating the report.

Reports run the gamut from ones that clients write themselves to more elaborate ones that we produce. On the cheap extreme, for a few projects we have agreed with the clients that at the end of the group work session we would leave them with the flip charts and that they would be responsible for putting together the report. We made sure that the clients had a clear sense of the order of the charts (numbered consecutively), each task that the group had done was distinct (titles in different colors on the flip charts made clear the beginning and ending of tasks), and that we were available to answer any questions while they compiled their report. An argument can be made that this approach is not only cost effective but also helps to build greater group ownership of the report and the work that it documents. For the facilitator, it clearly is one report that he or she will not have to write. On the down side, this approach means that someone in the client group may be spending more energy tracking activities than in participating in the meeting. It is also possible that the report will simply never be completed.

Certain technologies offer easy ways to document the meeting's accomplishments without writing a report. One way is to use a camera to take pictures of what was recorded on the boards or flip charts. The pictures can be placed in the files or copies of the photographs can be distributed. Color film will, of course, reproduce the different colors of ink that were used to capture ideas and highlight conclusions or title sections. Instant developing film will allow immediate turnaround. With newer technology, a video camera can record what went up on the boards or flip charts. We strongly advise against videotaping the whole meeting. Cameras tend to put some people off, leading them to participate less. Cameras also tend to bring out the ham in some people, leading them to play to the camera. The worst thing about taping the whole meeting is that you will have to watch the tapes. After having spent 8 to 16 hours with a group in its work sessions, you would then have to watch 8 to 16 hours of tape of the session. If you had taped all of the small groups you could have many more hours of tape to watch. The drudgery of viewing hours and hours of tape outweighs the benefit gained, at least in our view. (Justification can be made for taping if there is a research component to the work or if a video presentation is to be made about the project.)

Another option that helps avoid writing reports is to use the copy producing white boards to generate an instant report. These boards look like the dry-erase white boards that have been around for some time. These boards, however, incorporate a copier that generates letter size paper copies of what has been written on the board. Copies can be made for all participants before they leave. While these do not generate the different colors that were used on the board, they produce a black and white image of the material on the board. They reproduce the drawings, doodles, connecting arrows, text, strike-outs, and corrections. (If the meeting rooms have these boards you should use them even if it is only to generate copies for writing a traditional report.) Photographs or copy-generating white boards are ways to produce an instant documentation of the meeting in virtually a painless manner.

In most instances we develop some sort of report for the group using the information and decisions that they generated.

We do not write into the report what we think should have happened. We do not write the report from an "expert" point of view. We try to honestly reflect the actual content and process of what took place at the group meeting. We do not structure the report to follow the actual historically correct flow of the meeting. The report does clearly present the major elements and accomplishments of the group session. The outline for a full and lengthy report that we developed for a client is shown in Example 9.1. This report required between two to four full days to prepare. It was a relatively well-written document with narrative descriptions and introductions. It still would not communicate well to someone who had not been at the group work session the full richness of what had been done there.

We also generate more abbreviated reports that still convey the major decisions and actions the group appproved. Example 8.2 is a tabular display of the major group determinations taken from a report for the client. The total report ran only eight pages, including a title page and a page listing participants. For some clients who want us to generate a report but who also wish to keep the costs down as much as possible, we agree to produce a compilation of the meeting accomplishments. This means that we will produce a list of ideas, priorities, criteria, final decisions, and follow-through actions. This is far easier to write but is still historical documentation of what was done.

Using Recorders for Capturing
Meeting Accomplishments

When a team of facilitators operates a group work session it is easy to have some of the team serve as recorders. Recorders take down the short version of items listed on flip charts or white boards. They also try to get as much of the long version or explanation and context of the issues or comments as they are being presented. In some instances small groups will produce lists, guidelines, statements, and recommendations that are typed onto the computer and then printed out during the meeting for small and large group use.

Example 9.1 *Outline of a Facilitator-Generated Report*

I. Executive Summary: containing abbreviated versions of
   A. Action Plan
      1. Goals and objectives
      2. Actions to accomplish goals
      3. Time frame
      4. Resources needed
      5. Other issues
   B. Decisions Made
      1. To take action on specific issues
      2. To involve individuals or groups
      3. To report on results

II. Main Body of Report
   A. Action Plan
      1. Goals and objectives
      2. Actions to accomplish goals
      3. Time frame
      4. Resources needed
      5. Other issues
   B. Decisions Made
      1. To take action on specific issues
      2. To involve individuals or groups
      3. To report on results
   C. Meeting Purpose
   D. Issues and Topics Discussed
      1. Issues and context and discussion points
      2. Priority ideas listed about specific topics
   E. Brief description of the process used
      1. Facilitated meeting
      2. Collaborative involvement of groups members
      3. Ways of generating ideas
      4. Procedures/techniques for decision making
      5. Emphasis on group product in a structured setting

III. Appendixes
   A. Lists of ideas brainstormed or generated by the group (not
      identified with any specific individual or unit of the group)
   B. List of Participants
   C. Facilitator team members

It is our experience and luxury to have trained and competent recorders, most frequently using computers, at the community meetings we facilitate. We use recorders and computers for several reasons:

- for a record of activities, events, and decisions of the group;
- to produce conclusions, recommendations, and results for the group during the meeting; and
- to facilitate preparation of a report after the meeting.

The person recording on the computer, or in the low technology version on a pad of paper, does not identify who said what but provides a detailed description of the process and rationale by which the group arrived at consensus regarding issues and action plans. The facilitator who writes short comments on flip charts and the recorder who captures a more complete version must be careful to *use the words, language, and descriptions actually used by the participants.*

Using computers in the facilitated meeting means that it is very easy to list ideas and other items the group identified during the meeting. Group members can have a copy of their decision-making efforts or the results of small group brainstorming sessions as they attempt to integrate information and arrive at a commonly acceptable decision. Such lists and things printed during the meeting are not a substitute for a report, but they can greatly assist the group in its work. A quiet laser printer is a real asset during these sessions, because pages can be printed with a minimum of disruption.

Drafts and Revisions

When we write a report we are always sure to put a header on it or stamp it so that it is clearly marked as a DRAFT. That draft is sent out to the client. Our expectation is that a steering committee, review committee, or the full group will have a chance to read it, look for our errors, and offer suggestions. As a non-content expert the facilitator is able to remain neutral and outside of the group's discussions. This asset can become a liability during the report writing. It is easy to misunderstand a technical point or the way a word or phrase is used. By allowing the group to review the draft any mistakes can be corrected. Additionally, involving the group in reviewing the draft helps to raise the sense of ownership of the report.

The client can submit requests for changes to the report. These can be typing errors or misunderstandings on the part of the facilitation team in refinements or adjustments. Part of the alterations can be to make what could be misconstrued as a controversial statement less politically volatile. However, as facilitators we do not feel comfortable with and will resist changing the record to report something that did not actually happen. The changes submitted should lead to a more accurate documentation.

Who Owns the Report?

In our experience, facilitators provide the report to the client or group for their exclusive use. It is up to the client (unless otherwise specified in the contract) to duplicate and disseminate the report. Sometimes the contract or letter of agreement specifies that we will provide 50 or 100 copies of the report. In the design dance discussions we emphasize the idea of open meetings, including all interested and potentially impacted parties in the meeting, and to report results to the broader community via the news media, developing articles, and reports.

Admittedly, there have been times when we thought the client was "sitting" on the report, or wanted to rewrite the results to emphasize a special interest, or did not disseminate the group's efforts to its best advantage. Our position about these situations is that it is the groups' responsibility to use the report to accomplish their objectives. If the facilitator is invited back to review accomplishments, activities, and work on the action plan he or she may ask:

- How well was the report received in the community?
- Were newspaper articles helpful to accomplishing your objectives?
- Did individuals or groups volunteer to help accomplish some or all of the groups' objectives as indicated in the action plan?
- Was there any negative reaction or resistance to some of the objectives in the action plan?

Reports as Jumping-off Points

In a recent experience with a community we were asked to conduct a facilitated session and to help the group designate an action plan. This was not a brand new undertaking. The group was attempting to renew and reinvigorate an earlier planning effort. It was an added benefit that the group had a report from that community planning session. Group members reviewed, updated accomplishments, and set new directions for community improvement based upon the old report. Interestingly, two years after our work with this community client, another group was asked by the community to again review, update, and plan new activities (a third iteration). None of these events would have been as effective without a report from each of these earlier meetings.

FOLLOW-UP WITH CLIENT GROUPS

As facilitators we offer groups an optional benefit of meeting with them 3, 6 or 12 months later to review accomplishments toward action plans or objectives. At this time we are more in the role of asking questions about what they have done since the group work session or last meeting and what have they been able to do or change in the community or organization based upon their action plan. If given the follow-up opportunity, we also ask about what they plan to do in the future without the support of facilitators.

Follow-up is the area of work that may receive the least attention by the facilitator and the group. With the meeting project done, the action plan developed, an acceptable report finished and distributed, the group members are back at their regular jobs and responsibilities, it is easy to forget or put the action plan on the back burner. What should facilitators do?

The facilitator should remember:

- It is the group's agenda!
- It is the group's action plan!
- It is the group's responsibility to set the time frame for follow-up!

The facilitator can be helpful only if the group permits! One of the things facilitators can do is to volunteer to make periodic phone calls or visits to the community, agency, or group. An occasional call to the group leader asking if something could be done to be of assistance, about progress, next steps, and checking on the follow-up session can confirm interest in what the group is doing. A visit to meet with a subcommittee or selected group members to discuss an action agenda item can demonstrate interest in the group. During these informal meetings we like to point out how far the group has progressed and what it has accomplished. In some instances we may discuss ways of dividing a particular action or task into smaller, more doable parts.

In other situations, with other groups, follow-up is built into the groups' annual program. They start the year with a review and planning session. They review last year's plan and progress toward objectives. They identify what else needs to be done this coming year? Also, they look at what are the new issues or concerns and do they want to add more items to their action plan? One particular group we work with has been meeting annually for over three years, beginning with a group work session to plan the coming year's agenda. It seems to work for this group!

It is important to have a date, time, and location specified for the follow-up meeting 3, 6 or 12 months in the future. Someone will need to periodically keep the group informed of the meeting date, time, location, and work accomplished toward the plan. Perhaps this task can be assumed by a member of the group who has word processing, computer mail, and telecommunications resources.

At the follow-up meeting several months after the facilitated session, the facilitator can use such cuing questions as:

- What items on the plan were addressed?
- What new items have emerged?
- What has the group done?
- What else needs to be done?
- Have the goals been accomplished?
- Have the goals changed? How? Why?
- What are your next steps?

We believe it is important to look at the total effort of the group rather than to single out a few individuals or committees or small groups. Other individuals or small groups in the community may volunteer or be recruited to help in working on their items. It is important that their efforts are recognized and that they be incorporated into the larger group.

DISENGAGING FROM GROUPS

At some point in time groups must accept responsibility for their own development! Sometimes this is demonstrated by the group conducting annual or semiannual meetings or work sessions to review progress and need for new plans. In other situations the group may engage a different team of facilitators to help develop new action plans. Or a group may run out of steam by its own lack of action or commitment.

Disengagement is a learned process for both the facilitator and the group. Facilitators must develop processes, techniques, and methods to demonstrate for the groups how they, the clients, are in control and responsible for their own development. We hope that the more group members are involved actively in discussing *their* agenda and reaching consensus for options in *their* action plan, the more likely they are to commit *their* energy and time to taking control of *their* development.

A colleague of ours was asked how he knew when we had done good work in a community? What did he use to evaluate his and our performance? He replied that when the local news-paper writes a report about the group meeting and the results of that meeting, if the consultants are not mentioned at all or only mentioned in the very last paragraph, then we have been success-ful. This may or may not be a measure of total success or effec-tiveness. The absence of the facilitator being highlighted in local press coverage is at least an indicator of local or client ownership of the product. It also points to a good start on successful disen-gaging by the consultant.

Perhaps more attention should be directed toward helping groups learn how to take charge of their action plans. Our ex-perience along this line is to look at the action plan realistically and ask for commitment to work on a part (or all parts) of a specific item or activity that is doable in a relatively short period of time . . . say 3 to 6 months. We work hard to establish a pro-cess where groups members can determine what *they* want to happen, designate what *they* want to work on, and have control over the time frame to do the job.

Related to taking control of their action plan, is recognition of the group and members for working hard and accomplishing an objective. Often this process of recognition is overlooked and it appears that the same few people seem to show up and do most of the work. By getting all of the players to the table to discuss issues and reach consensus on actions it is likely that more people will work toward their agreed upon interests.

SUMMARY

The after phase of the facilitation process is all about hand-ing off the project to the group. The entire approach of facilita-tion as we envision it and as we discuss it in the book is as a process for helping to involve the client in the negotiation, the design of the process, the deliberations and discussions at the session, and finally moving to implementation. This last phase attempts to complete this handing off. Putting the report into the group members' hands gives them a record they can consult. Being on retainer and available to come back for a follow-up meeting provides an important resource for the client to call upon. The follow-up meeting is an opportunity to reassemble the group, check on progress, help to revise plans, and reenergize and motivate. The intent is to disengage from this particular intervention and in the long run raise the abilities of the clients so that they can attempt to handle some of these things on their own.

CHAPTER 10

Conclusion

There are two primary reasons why one ought to facilitate groups. The first reason is on the short-term time frame. In the near-term a facilitator is able to assist a group in confronting a problem and devising a means for dealing with it. The key here is that a facilitative approach is often able to overcome the limitations encountered by the expert consultant. The facilitator can help the group to arrive at its definition of its problem, to generate its ideas about how to address the problem, to select an idea to pursue, and to build an action agenda or implementation scheme for follow-through. Facilitation is designed to build group ownership in the ideas, the agreements, the decisions, and the product. In the short term one facilitates a group because it is an approach that seems to enable a group to come to a common understanding, agree on a course of action, and build momentum for group action. Facilitation is used because it helps to bring about change.

In the long term facilitation is a preferred way to operate because it slowly but surely empowers the group. A delayed benefit to the group is that there is a technology transfer going on that is not usually an explicit part of the contract between facilitator and client. The client group is brought to appreciate what a facilitator can do, how a group can be helped, and when facilitation might be beneficial. Additionally, techniques and approaches can be transferred from the facilitator to the clients so that they become able to operate without the facilitator, but at a level of competence that they did not have before. In some cases the facilitator may train members of the client group to serve as small group facilitators. In these cases there is a direct technology transfer by the facilitator to the client and the community. In the long term the facilitator can raise the awareness and abilities of the client group.

The reasons for facilitating community and decision-making groups essentially have to do with the fact that it works for the client. It works in the long term and in the short term. It works for the consultant as well, because it gets one out of the role of an expert telling people the technically correct solution and then watching that solution rarely get enacted.

HOW TO GET STARTED

You can understand everything there is to know about facilitating a group. You can be familiar with the concepts. You can comprehend what facilitation is and is not. But that knowledge by itself is not enough. What you must do is, try it! You must experience it to really bring it all together. Facilitation, like riding a bicycle, is one of those things that you need to do in order to really learn it.

Getting the Chance to Facilitate

As in too many cases where experience counts, you may find it hard to acquire the first bit of experience. You may run up against people who are not willing to be your guinea pigs in order for you to gain your experience. This is reasonable from their point of view but frustrating for you. The easiest way to begin acquiring experience is in small stages. You can start by attending facilitated meetings as a participant. At these meetings you can keep yourself from becoming entirely consumed by the discussion and content and remain aware of the group process and what the facilitator does and does not do. At the end of the session you can approach the facilitator and determine if he or she is receptive to discussion and questions about what has been done. Watching others practice their craft will allow you to see the major strategies that are used and the approaches that can be taken. It will also sensitize you to what you will need to do as a facilitator.

In the continuing acquisition of experience you can work with a facilitation team as a recorder. You can volunteer to act as the recorder of either a small break-out group or for the entire group. This will mean that all of your attention will be focused on the flow and process of the group in its work. Rather than being a participant who is waiting to get in your own comments and stealing an occasional opportunity to observe the facilitator, you will be watching and recording the work of the group as it is guided by the facilitator. Because you will be providing a valuable service to the facilitator you will be in position to bargain for some debriefing time, advice, and the opportunity to gain more experience.

A nice entry point for actually trying to facilitate is as the facilitator of a small break-out group at a larger group session. As one of a team of group facilitators you can expect to be advised about what exactly is expected of your group and what procedure you are to use. Typically this will be a constrained and manageable task and a session that is rather short, no more than a couple of hours. This opportunity can be incredibly valuable. You have the chance to try out what you have learned. You have the chance to speak with other small group facilitators and compare experiences. You may have the chance to work with a recorder in your session and to receive feedback later from that person. You may also have the chance to be observed by the lead facilitator and get that person's perceptions of what and how you did. The best thing about this experience is that it will be a relatively low risk operation. The success or failure of the entire group work session will not be riding upon your shoulders alone.

Debriefing and talking to an observer about what you did and how you came across is most valuable. It is also very useful to observe others and talk to them about what they did. Ask them why they tried certain techniques, what they were trying to do when they turned a certain way or used a hand gesture, why they deviated from a predetermined plan of action with the group, and why they didn't try something.

Continue to practice. Identify groups that could benefit

from a facilitator and work with them. Find a mentor or an experienced facilitator team to work with. Facilitation is not a science. There is not a set of theories or firm methodologies that you learn and then know it all. It is also not an art whose successful execution is dependent upon an intuitive sense of balance, color, composition, and so on. Facilitation is a craft. It has elements of science. These scientific elements are the truths revealed by research about group process or the knowledge about structured methods for approaching different types of problems. It also has elements of art. These are best reflected by the times when you must go with your feelings about how a group session is developing or what a group needs. With experience and practice you will get better and better at integrating these elements into your practice of facilitation.

Training Programs

An alternative approach to gaining additional knowledge and experience is to attend a training session on facilitation. Our advice is for you to be sure to attend a training session that is heavy on experiential learning. While you cannot be harmed by acquiring additional information, what you need most is experience. You should take the risk, get up in front of a group, practice facilitation, and receive some feedback. A well-run training program will provide you with exactly that mix of learning experiences. These programs are offered by a variety of institutions. Look for one that is convenient, cost-effective, and has a good reputation.

THINGS TO REMEMBER

Several things come to mind that are worthy of restatement or of reemphasis at this point. These are fundamentals that ought to be remembered when we facilitate community and decision-making groups. First, have faith in the process. Have faith in the wisdom and ability of groups to explore their own situations and to craft strategies for solving their own problems. We believe that groups, with some assistance, can decide what they want to do and develop action plans to accomplish their goals. Many existing groups do this on a continuing basis. We find our services needed most often by zero-history groups or by groups that have an especially difficult, emotional, or value laden problem to solve. Specifying, what we can and cannot do in the design dance helps to inform people about our resources and skills to assist the groups in solving their own problems.

Second, the groups ought to establish their expectations and concerns for the agenda. It is their agenda! Facilitators are aggressive about selecting specific techniques, strategies, and procedures for the group to use in problem solving. This is the unique contribution of the facilitator! But the facilitator's techniques and abilities must be directed to helping the groups surface and then address their own agendas.

Third, in order to perform the facilitator role, the facilitator must "leave his or her ego at the door." It is the group's agenda, the group's problem, the group's solution, the group's action plan, and the group's responsibility to implement the action plan! In order for the facilitators to help the group in this effort they must be secure enough to allow their own self-worth to be defined by something other than what the group decides. The facilitators' egos must be out of the way of the group's deliberations.

Fourth, keeping the ego in check can also help to prevent the facilitator from becoming the expert. There is no room in this experience for the facilitators to impose their values, expertise, or superior knowledge upon the group. Just because you may know something about the issue, for example, managing and protecting wetlands, does not give you the right to be the expert authority for the group. A facilitator who suddenly acts in the expert role is perceived by the group as an expert and is very seldom, if ever, able to shake the perception of expert and resume an effective facilitator role. If the facilitator feels that it is crucial to share some knowledge with the client group, the switch of roles from facilitator to expert and then back again, must be done very openly and explicitly. The facilitator can announce that he or she is putting on a different hat for a few minutes to share some specific piece of information and then announce a return to the neutral role. Until a facilitator has gained some experience and confidence it is best to avoid these shifts in role and not confuse the group and him- or herself.

Fifth, when speaking, and especially when writing on flip charts, newsprint, and white boards be sure to use the language of the group. If someone in the group mentions a concern for recreation, the facilitator needs to use that term rather than "sports fitness" or "health promotion" or some other term. Group members should see what they said rather than having to translate the language or jargon of the facilitator. Using their words helps to build that sense of ownership.

Sixth, take time to involve all group members throughout the process. Using such techniques as brainstorming, nominal group technique (NGT), and brainwriting offers multiple opportunities for members to express their concerns. These concerns often relate to issues, problems, and possible solutions. If it is their problem and they have contributed to identifying possible solutions, it is likely they will want to assume ownership and work toward that solution.

Seventh, facilitators need to know if the group is working toward its expectations and goals for the meeting. Periodic checking in with the group is necessary to affirm " . . . is this the direction you want to go?" " . . . are we addressing the issue you believe are most important?" " . . . have we taken this approach or solution as far as we can go for now?" " . . . do you want to spend some time discussing this issue?"

Eighth, the facilitator must remember and help the group to remember that the success of a facilitated group work session depends upon both parties playing their parts. The facilitator and the client must both play their roles for the experience to work. If the session goes well, both parties need to give themselves credit. Similarly, if things do not work out well (and sometimes they do not) both parties need to take the blame. This last point is key. It is very easy for facilitators to credit a group when things go well but to blame themselves when things do not work out. Success and failure are the results of shared responsibilities.

Ninth, remember that as you work with groups, they want to succeed. At least, the vast majority of people in the group want to succeed. As challenging as it may seem at times, the clients want you to do a good job and want you to help them to do good work. This is a valuable asset to use as you work as a facilitator with community and decision-making groups.

Finally, you need to be honest with yourself about your ability to act as a facilitator. Be ready to admit to yourself that facilitation may not be for you. Not everyone is cut out to be a facilitator. If it happens that you are one of these people, that is just the way it is. This does not mean that you are not a good person or a valuable person. It just means that you should focus your energies on things you are better at doing. We had one person in one of our training sessions who at the end of the session grinned at us and said that he now knew that he did not ever want to facilitate. We thought of that as a very positive outcome for this person. We hope that you will be honest with yourself and decide whether facilitation is for you. If it is for you, welcome to the challenge!

APPENDIX

Sample Contract

Purpose

Noname County, the Main City, and other incorporated cities face a future which presents significant challenges but which also provides opportunities for positive growth and enhancement of the community. The Chamber of Commerce, the County, City, and other community leaders have recognized the need to confront the challenges and the opportunities of the future by undertaking a community planning process to ensure quality growth. As a provider of technical assistance to communities and areas of the state, the Organization is in a unique position to offer help in this planning effort through a process of "decision conferencing."

The Organization proposes to work with a broad spectrum of community leaders from the public, private, and not-for-profit sectors to identify the desired future for this area and to begin charting a course for achieving that future. With the Organization's facilitation, the community leadership will develop a plan that the community can embrace and apply broadly. The end product of the planning process will be a document which contains the essential actions which need to be taken by the community to realize quality growth and the sort of future desired by the community. This will then serve as the framework for the ongoing community effort to work for the desired future.

Methods

The Organization will employ its expertise and staff resources in the planning process to ensure the successful planning for Noname County and the cities' future. The Organization staff will interview each of the community leaders selected to participate in the strategic planning process. It will be the responsibility of the County, City, and Chamber to ensure that the selected participants are as representative as possible of the entire community while not exceeding approximately thirty (30) in number. The Organization staff will use a variety of interview techniques, including open-ended questioning as well as closed-ended survey instruments. The interviewing is an important and essential component of the process which allows the Organization to gain a sense of the sort of future desired for the area and prepare for the decision conference so as to ensure that maximum use of the participants' time is made.

The Organization staff will conduct a full two-day session for the community leaders at which the community plan will be developed. The Organization will employ a "computer-assisted decision conference" approach to assist the group in the development of the plan. This approach to group decision making is designed to maximize participant involvement through discussion and consensus building. The approach makes the greatest possible use of participants' time and knowledge while freeing them of the necessity to keep a record of the progress and attempting to integrate large volumes of disparate information. The Organization uses a structured approach to facilitate the group in laying out the plan. The approach makes intensive use of Organization personnel as group facilitators and recorders to see that the session achieves the desired objective and that a running record of all information and decisions is maintained to document the work of the planning session. The Organization will employ computers and software to integrate and analyze the information presented by participants and the deliberations of the small work groups.

Deliverables

The Organization will provide the following products and services to the Countywide Chamber of Commerce and governments:

1. *Interviews with the Leaders Who Will Participate in the Planning Effort.* The Organization staff will conduct an interview with each participant to determine what he or she feels to be the major challenges facing the community. The participants will be asked to speak candidly and confidentially about their concerns. Open-ended questions will be used to determine individuals' perceptions; in addition a closed-ended questionnaire will also be used. The information gathered in these interviews will allow the Organization to structure the group session and tentatively plan the topics of the small work groups to which the participants will be assigned. *It is imperative that each of the participants be willing to devote one hour prior to the work session for the administration of the survey and for the open-ended interview.*

2. *Decision Conference for Community Leaders.* This session should be held over two days at a location removed from the normal day-to-day activities of the participants. The participants should be an invited set of approximately thirty (30) people representing the diverse interests and groups of the community. They should include the business community, education, government, not-for-profit organizations, citizen groups, and so on.

The decision conference will be an intensive working session for all of the participants. It will begin with a presentation of the results of the survey and interviews. This will provide the framework within which all of the work of the next two days will occur. The rest of the day will focus on the process of "model building." This model building process consists of a structured approach to decision making which asks participants to provide all of the information in a logical step-by-step procedure. The decision-structuring technique will be made clear to all of the participants. The participants will then be broken out into small groups to begin identifying the actions which need to be taken to ensure quality growth within their assigned topic area, as well as estimates of the costs and benefits of those actions.

The second day of the group session will allow the small groups to finish any loose ends, but will be primarily concerned with integrating the work of all the small groups into an overall model. At this stage, the actions identified in each topic area are combined into a structured plan, and the participants will fine tune the model by asking "what if" questions and revising earlier estimates. The goal is not to devise a detailed plan, but to outline the major elements: what needs to be done, the resources needed to accomplish what is desired, and the benefit that is expected to accrue to the community. The computer model is used to integrate the information and suggest a reasonable ordering of all of the many actions suggested for assuring quality growth and the desired future.

At the conclusion of the second day, participants will set an agenda for follow-up activities. Typically, a small group of participants work to refine the cost and benefit estimates in the model and review the steps in the model.

3. *Summary of the Decision Conference.* The Organization will deliver to the County, Cities, and Chamber, not later than two weeks following the conclusion of the conference, a written record of the group's work. The document will be a summary of the work accomplished. It will present the model in the final version as agreed to by the participants. It will incorporate the rationale for important decisions made in the development of the plan and the building of the model. This document will serve as the framework for the full and detailed plans for implementing the vision of the future that was developed by the community leaders who participated in the group session.

4. *Subsequent Steps.* The Organization will be available to the Chamber and the Noname County community to assist in follow through. It is recommended that all group participants attend a one-half day work session approximately six (6) months later in order to review and evaluate the progress made. It is also recommended that such sessions be held annually thereafter.

Project Coordination

The Organization will designate an individual staff member to serve as the project director. The project director will assign experienced staff to assist in the completion of each of the stages of the project. The Organization will require an individual in the community to be designated as the coordinator to assist in scheduling the interviews, identifying sources of local information, etc.

Timetable

The work program outlined above will take approximately three months to complete. The decision conference can be held four to six weeks after the start of the project. The remaining time can be used for refinement of the work done at the group session and modifying the model and the report.

Budget

The Organization will provide the service for the sum of $X,000. This fee will cover such direct costs as travel, per diem expenses during the interview phase, computer analysis, printing, and use of special equipment for the decision conference. Subsidized personnel costs for the Organization staff will be contributed by the Organization.

At the decision conference, Noname County, each of the incorporated cities, and the Chamber of Commerce will be responsible for the Organization staff's lodging and meal costs (in addition to the $X,000 charge). Approximately seven (7) to ten (10) Organization staff members will be needed to conduct the decision conference.

It is also suggested that the expenses of the community members participating in the conference be underwritten by the Chamber, the cities, and Noname County.

REFERENCES

Adams, J. L. (1979). *Conceptual blockbusting: Agenda to better ideas* (2nd ed.). New York: W. W. Norton.

Ashby, W. R. (1958). Requisite variety and its implications for the control of complex systems. *Cybernetics*, 1, 1–17.

Birkey, C. J. M. (1984). Future directions for adult education and adult educators. *Journal of Teacher Education*, 35(3), 25–29.

Bostrom, R. P., Anson, R., & Clawson, V. (1991). Group facilitation and group support systems. *Group support systems: New Perspectives* (pp. 1–48). In L. Jessup & J. Valacick (Eds.), New York: Van Nostrand.

Brookfield, S. C. (1986). *Understanding and facilitating adult learning: A comprehensive analysis of principles and effective practices.* San Francisco: Jossey-Bass.

Carver, J. (1990). *Boards that make a difference.* San Francisco: Jossey-Bass.

Corey, G., Corey, M. S., Callanan, P. J., & Russell, J. M. (1988). *Group techniques.* Pacific Grove, CA: Brooks/Cole Publishing Company.

Delbecq, A. L., Van de Ven, A. H., & Gustafson, D. H. (1975). *Group techniques for program planning.* Glenview, IL: Scott Foresman and Company.

Dimock, H. (1987). *Groups: Leadership and group development.* San Diego: University Associates.

Fisher, B. A., & Ellis, D. G. (1990). *Small group decision making.* New York: McGraw-Hill.

Forbess-Greene, S. (1983). *The encyclopedia of icebreakers: Structured activities that warm-up, motivate, challenge, acquaint and energize.* San Diego: University Associates.

Friend, J., & Hickling, A. (1987). *Planning under pressure: The strategic choice approach.* New York: Pergamon Press.

Galbraith, M. W. (1991). Preface. In M. W. Galbraith (Ed.), *Facili-

tating adult learning: A transactional process (pp. ix-xii). Malabar, FL: Krieger.

Gordon, W. J. (1961). *Synectics*. New York: Harper and Row.

Heron, J. (1989). *The facilitators handbook*. London: Kogan Page, Ltd.

Huber, G. P. (1980). *Managerial decision making*. Glenview, IL: Scott, Foresman and Company.

Kayser, T. A. (1990). *Mining group gold*. El Segundo, CA: Serif.

McGrath, J. E. (1984). *Groups: Interaction and performance*. Englewood Cliffs: Prentice-Hall.

Nutt, P. C. (1989). *Making tough decisions*. San Francisco: Jossey-Bass.

Rees, F. (1991). *How to lead work teams: Facilitation skills*. San Diego: Pfeiffer & Company.

Steele, F. I. (1973). *Physical settings and organization development*. Reading, MA: Addison-Wesley.

Thomas, K. W., & Kilmann, R. H. (1974). *Thomas-Kilmann conflict mode instrument*. Tuxedo, NY: Xicom.

University Associates (1972–1991). Annual series of handbooks for facilitators of developing human resources (titles have changed over the course of the series). San Diego: University Associates.

VanGundy, A. B. (1984). *Managing group creativity*. New York: American Management Associations.

VanGundy, A. B. (1988). *Techniques of structured problem solving* (2nd ed.). New York: Van Rostrand Reinhold.

Volkema, R. (1983). Problem formulation planning and design. *Management Science*. 28(6), 639–652.

Webster's Seventh New College Dictionary (1972). Springfield, MA: G&C Merriam Company.

Wheelan, S. A. (1990). *Facilitating training groups*. New York: Praeger Publishers.

Whorton, J. W. (1993). Developing effective community groups. In R. Golembiewski, R. (Ed.), *Handbook of organizational consultation*. New York: Marcel Dekker.

Wilson, G. L., & Hanna, M. S. (1990). *Groups in context: Leadership and participation in small groups*. New York: McGraw-Hill.

INDEX